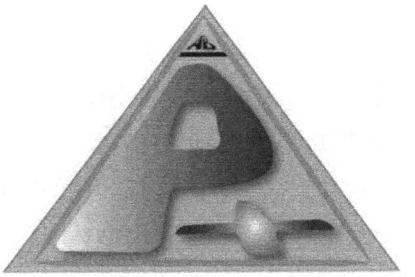

Other Titles By Gary Younglove

Tools: For Spike And Nails
Sing Me No Sad Songs
Phantom Memories:
In Search Of Thunderbird F4Es
Groan And Bear It

Vision To Reality:

A Brief History of

Fair Oaks Ranch, Texas

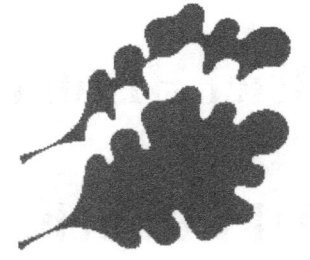

Dedication

To Piper Kate Younglove

And

All the Residents of Fair Oaks Ranch

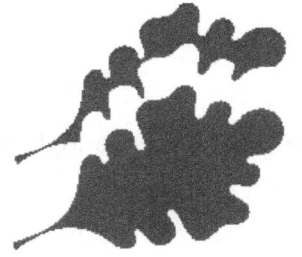

Vision To Reality:

A Brief History Of

Fair Oaks Ranch, Texas

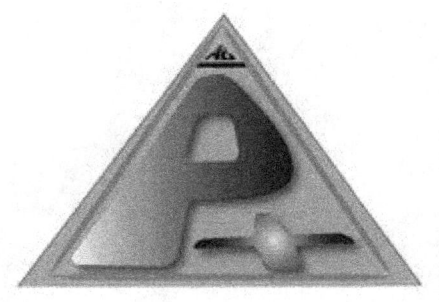

Piper Plus Publications

Vision To Reality:

A Brief

History

Of

Fair Oaks Ranch, Texas

By

Gary D. Younglove

Vision To Reality:

A Brief History Of Fair Oaks Ranch, Texas

Orders@PiperPlusPublications.com
Shipping Information On Website
http://www.PiperPlusPublications.com
Piper Plus Publications
28540 Jim Dandy Circle
Fair Oaks Ranch, TX 78015

**Also available in eBook format from:
Amazon Kindle and Barnes and Noble Nook**

Copyright © 2013 by Gary Younglove

All rights reserved. No part of this book may be reproduced or transmitted in any form or by any means, electronic or mechanical, including photocopying, recording, or by any information storage and retrieval system, without written permission from the author except for the inclusion of brief quotations in a review.

ISBN: 978-0-9829383-8-6

Library of Congress Control Number: 2013930102

eBook ISBN: 978-0-9829383-7-9

10 9 8 7 6 5 4 3 2

ACKNOWLEDGEMENTS

This book would not have been possible without the actions of the founding fathers when Fair Oaks Ranch was only a place too far from San Antonio, Texas, that big city to the south, to be of interest to anyone. In that regard, Erwin "Boots" Gaubatz, Don King, and Brigadier General Robert Herring deserve a lion's share of the thanks.

Ralph Fair, Jr., Bob Weiss, and Don Smith also deserve their own sincere thanks for the community spirit, selfless support for the incorporation effort, and continuing partnership in making the administration of Fair Oaks Ranch a successful government entity. Their integrity and generosity were major factors in this achievement.

To the many individuals who volunteered their time in interviews or in response to my many questions, I also give thanks. Of special note are Ralph Fair, Jr., Bob Weiss, Don Smith, Robert Herring, Dan Kasprowicz, and David Deleranko.

Special thanks go to Mayor Cheryl Landman, Roy Thomas, Carole Vanzant, and Linda Zartler who provided editorial support and historical scrutiny of the events included. Without their review of the manuscript and concise input and corrections concerning the events related, this book would be much less than it is.

Finally, my thanks to the Aldermen of the Fair Oaks Ranch City Council who agreed to take the chance that I could write something useful.

FOREWORD

To be a participant in the formation of a "new city" creates a personal ownership like none other. The City of Fair Oaks Ranch, once a five thousand acre working Texas ranch, began its development in the late 1980s although the ranch itself began in the mid-1970s. Today, it is my humble privilege to serve as Mayor for approximately six thousand citizens and oversee approximately eight thousand acres within the City and the surrounding area.

This book commemorates the 25th Anniversary of our City and provides an insider's look at how a simple Texas ranch became a self-directed city. Gary Younglove, the author, brings depth to this story with both his historical insights and wordsmithing! From a personal perspective, Gary stands tall at about 6'2", is a retired military officer with a tour on the USAF Thunderbirds one of his many highlights, a biker, husband, father, and grandfather of triplets, an author of four books and a most caring protector of nature with bird-watching and a 1,500 foot nature trail on his land that serves as a special hobby. Working with Gary who sat on the Council for many years, I thought I knew him. Only recently did he reveal that he holds a degree in Theology. He also built the City's first website and computer network and even wrote the City's mission. Never one to wait for direction, he has continued his efforts to make this City great and was honored as the Volunteer of the Year in 2010. Some have called Gary a modern day renaissance man. There seems to be nothing he can't do. You will find Gary's personal ownership weaves a spell binding tale!

There are many families from the 1970s still living here and each one adds their unique personal ownership to the City's development. Over the years, many new residents have made Fair Oaks Ranch their home of choice. Those moving in come from all over the United States as well as outside the USA. The City culture and the many life-style opportunities entice them; this book explains why and how today's coveted culture began and grew to be their home of choice. They too will create their own personal ownership.

You, the reader, will understand how certain decisions made since the 1970s - often under heavy debate - still provide the roadmap to success for the City of Fair Oaks Ranch. For instance, in the earlier years this looked more like a retirement area. Today, with the donation of land by the developer, Ralph Fair, Inc., to build an elementary school in the City, it is now a balanced community with families of all ages. Interestingly, many of the elementary school students are the grandchildren of our more mature residents.

Another twist is that often the family is here first and then come the grandparents. Preparing for this type of projected growth over the next eight to ten years, the school district purchased additional land in the city for a second elementary school about five years ago. Since 1978, the original Fair family's 1930s ranch home has served as the center for the Fair Oaks Ranch Golf and Country Club (FORGCC). The original 14,000 square foot home has expanded to almost 22,000 square feet under the management of CLUBCORP. Golf and tennis are strong draws for both the current and incoming residents. *AvidGolfer* magazine voted the club as The Best Overall Family Value Country Club for three years running.

I refer to our city as "urban-rural" as at one time it was all rural. The original homesteads developed in the early 1970s are "ranchettes" of ten – twenty acres each where residents today enjoy their privacy and their horses. Yes, there are those caution signs for "deer crossing" as well as "horse crossing". With approximately 12 miles dedicated to private greenbelt trails throughout the city, one often sees horse riders as well as walkers and bicyclists.

As you begin your read, Gary takes you back much further than the original Fair ranch. Yet the evidence of this pre-historic beginning is noted with copious relics of the past under the land. I understand from some of the older families in the area that their kids would come and play on the ranch…with permission of course…who, now grown to adulthood, still covet the copious arrowheads found when the Fair's decided to dig down for a swimming pool addition.

The personal ownership I feel toward the City of Fair Oaks

Ranch runs deep and is captured by Gary's work as the rural ranch vision becomes the reality of an urban-rural city. We are still moving forward and growing always mindful of what a unique place this is to each resident.

Enjoy!

Cheryl Landman, Mayor
City of Fair Oaks Ranch, Texas
My personal "Camelot" since 1987.

PREFACE

Writing a history of Fair Oaks Ranch was a challenge for me. The two year effort was interrupted by a number of real life issues I had to deal with. And the effort to keep from referring to myself in the narrative too frequently ended up with me referring to 'the Council' on many occasions. I was involved in the beginning of the City and remained a participant in its growth for sixteen years. Keeping my memories of what 'went down' according to many reports versus what 'really happened' according to many witnesses required diligence. Then reporting what 'is fact' according to official documents provided many conflicts to resolve and I often wondered if I was up to the task. But I had committed to the task when Mayor Cheryl Landman asked me to write this book for the 25th Fair Oaks Ranch Anniversary Celebration. I could not refuse. And as it turned out, it was an enjoyable experience.

Fair Oaks Ranch remains a unique place to live in spite of all that has taken place since its beginning in 1986. I use 1986 and not the commonly accepted birthdate of 1988 because the City was in all actuality conceived in the Sons Of Hermann Hall on Dietz Elkhorn Road with the vote of the homeowners in attendance there in November 1986. As they say: All after that is history.

The only significant difficulty I faced when writing this book was selecting what would be included. This is not a comprehensive history of everything that took place as the City grew. Such a recording in words would result in a document of untenable boredom. All cities face similar issues such as administration and street maintenance and Council debates. Fair Oaks Ranch was not immune to these issues. But it is not the purpose of this book to cover every one of the mundane actions involved in the City's operation. I tried to cover only those events and happenings that had a significant impact on the City's founding, formation, and growth into a mature government.

I am quietly proud of my part in the growth of this development into a city and a fully functioning government entity. Many whom I worked with on the City Council and in the voluntary organizations cooperating with the City are no longer with us. Both the Mayors of the two cities that became one, Boots Gaubatz and Don King, have gone from us with unexpected rapidity. Don Smith, the person Ralph Fair, Jr. enlisted to develop the 'Ranch' into a community, departed only very recently. What we see now is the product of these visionaries' dreams – dreams that have come true. They would be proud of how their efforts have played out and we should respect their work. They were committed, dedicated, honorable, and continuously in search of what was best for the community. I salute them. As should all the residents of the City.

Fair Oaks Ranch continues to be a magnet for people wanting to escape the restrictions of other communities and whose desires include a country atmosphere, limited government, and freedom. That concept, freedom, was my driving motivation when I served on the Council. Sometimes my commitment to the concept of free choice conflicted with others on the Council as well as residents who wanted some special action that fit their agenda. It is a credit to Fair Oaks Ranch that we always worked out the differences to the benefit of all.

My family and I have lived and moved and created new lives and moved again and again so many times that we felt like nomads. We were finally blessed with the final move to Fair Oaks Ranch. I found my country place and I stopped looking for anything else. My Camelot is right here. Many residents of Fair Oaks Ranch feel the same way. There are few, if any, cities that come close to what our Camelot has achieved. And based on the continued volunteer involvement of the leadership in both the City and the Fair Oaks Ranch Homeowners Association, I doubt that any will ever come close.

Fair Oaks Ranch, Texas, is a special place. For most of us living here, life is good.

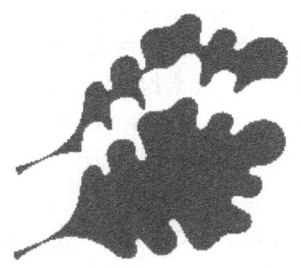

CONTENTS

Acknowledgements

Foreword

Preface

Introduction

PART ONE – THE FOUNDATION

> Chapter One: The Geological Base
> Chapter Two: The Ecological Base
> Chapter Three: The Anthropological Base

PART TWO – THE FORMATION

> Chapter Four: Common Sense Government
> Chapter Five: Visionary Thinking Wins
> Chapter Six: A Little Home Schooling
> Chapter Seven: The Census Don't Know
> Chapter Eight: One Plus One = One

PART THREE – THE FOLLOW-THROUGH

> Chapter Nine: Setting Up House
> Chapter Ten: Don't Mess With Fair Oaks Ranch

Chapter Eleven: Support Your Local Sheriff
Chapter Twelve: Oh My Dear
Chapter Thirteen: A Bridge Over Troubled Waters

PART FOUR – THE FAMILY FEUDS

Chapter Fourteen: Movin' On Up To The East Side
Chapter Fifteen: Business Ain't Doing So Well
Chapter Sixteen: Water, Water, Everywhere
Chapter Seventeen: Making Water Flow Uphill
Chapter Eighteen: AC/DC

PART FIVE – THE FUTURE

Chapter Nineteen: Wrapping It Up
Chapter Twenty: Things to Come

Epilog

APPENDICES

Volunteers

Council Members And Periods Of Service

Fair Oaks Ranch Statistics

References

INTRODUCTION

... Oh, somewhere in this favored land the sun is shining bright;
The band is playing somewhere, and somewhere hearts are light,
And somewhere men are laughing, and somewhere children shout; ...

Ernest Thayer wrote those words in 1888 as part of his poem 'Casey At The Bat'.[1] And those words aptly describe a special *somewhere* in Texas - specifically in South Central Texas on the southeastern edge of what the locals call the Hill Country. Longtime resident Erwin 'Boots' Gaubatz, one of the founders and the first mayor of this *somewhere* community, believed it was as close to Camelot as you can get. Besides being in the United States of America, which is a singular benefit in and of itself, this community is in Texas - the proverbial icing on the cake. Just ask anyone who lives here. We like Texas. We like being in Texas. And when we travel we like saying we're from Texas. Live here long enough and you will come to understand that Texas is, after all, not just a State in the Union of States. It is primarily a state of mind.

On a more regionally focused basis chances are you will be hard pressed to find anyone who doesn't speak well of the Texas Hill Country and few who don't speak highly of the small City of Fair Oaks Ranch – a city with the unique status of lying in three separate and fundamentally different counties. This South Central Texas Camelot is a place where the sun is always shining bright and hearts are always light. It is a place that is one of the youngest cities in Texas and one of the most desirable places in the area to make your home.

This book is a record of selected events that make up the core issues the City of Fair Oaks Ranch faced during its march to maturity. It attempts to tell what makes this place special - that place known as *somewhere* as Ernest Thayer says - and cover the most significant events that make it a model city. The first 25 years of this City's existence has been filled with a multitude of successes amid its spectacular growth. It has become what others who wish to form their own city and control their own destiny use as an example of how to do it right. But, as this story will relate, the City was very nearly stillborn and had to overcome some serious challenges even before it could get out of the crib into the playroom.

Located about 25 miles north by northwest of the famed Alamo in the heart of San Antonio, Texas, Fair Oaks Ranch is nestled in the rolling, predominately live oak covered hills that form the Hill Country's apron. In 1970, what was to eventually become a city was a 5,000 acre ranch that was considered somewhat remote from the San Antonio metropolis to its south. Known then as the Fair Ranch, it was just a few miles south of the quiet and, at the time, undiscovered City of Boerne, an old German community established in 1852 during the influx of immigrants arriving from the old country.[2] The only access to the ranch was up a narrow Farm to Market road known as FM 3351 that bordered the U.S. Army Camp Bullis and Camp Stanley to the east. You could not see the ranch from Interstate Highway 10, the major artery running from California to Florida and back that carved its way through these rolling hills just a mile west of the ranch.

For many years it lay in this secluded location - known to only a few. However, it was a thriving operational ranch of some note to those in the business of ranching. Acquired piece by piece in the 'thirties', the 'Ranch' changed missions over the years but never as much as what happened in the 70s. The changes that took place then were destined to alter the landscape (literally and figuratively) forever. The remote area unnoticed by travelers going east or west on IH 10 was to become a vanguard of community success that many would emulate. That success is continuing to grow day after day. And the City that grew from humble beginnings that were often considered experimental is now known throughout the region as a symbol of community cohesiveness.

To adequately grasp the basis of the success this city has enjoyed, it is helpful to understand a handful of things about the region and the City's specific location. The initial chapters to this book in *Part One - The Foundation* provide a background of factors that help in understanding why the area is so enticing to those who choose to live here. The story goes back millions of years when what we now know as Texas was buried first under mountains and then under seas. The geological, ecological, and anthropological facets of Texas' history are fundamental to the formation of what eventually becomes a city.

In *Part Two - The Formation* you will find the details of how a small group of men and a supportive and crucially important developer joined hands to provide the necessary partnership to ensure success. Facing deadlines and uncertainties, these men persevered and a new city was formed on principles that have withstood the usual attacks when a bold approach is tried. The nearly failed attempt to avoid annexation by San Antonio is almost classic in itself.

Part Three - The Follow Through will discuss many of the challenges the newly formed city faced while trying to exercise its mission of minimal government and fiscal responsibility. Low taxes, full services, hands-off government, individual responsibility, common sense involvement - these were all part of the original mission that still stands unchanged from the very beginning and has become a trademark of the City.

In *Part Four – The Family Feuds* a few of the most controversial issues facing the young city are covered. Things were not always as smooth and beautiful as the Camelot descriptor would have you believe. There were differences in how things should be run and what things should be allowed.

And *Part Five – The Future* looks ahead at what is planned and the challenges that arise from growth - too much of a good thing can bring with it changes not planned for in the beginning. The City faces events and circumstances that could alter its time honored position in ways never envisioned by its founders.

In all this, the Texas Hill Country attitude prevails. The inheritors of the freedoms granted by a local government whose founders followed a vision of being as minimally intrusive as possible while providing all the things citizens expect from a community remains the pivotal leverage of success. It is as it should be: there when you need it - absent when you don't.

You will discover many things about the City that are known by only a few people involved with its birth and growth. Many tales of interest will be presented that will hopefully help explain why the City is so special. Perhaps the telling of this history will help someone find a way to make their community similarly successful. The core of the City's being is also its most notable accomplishment - volunteer citizen participation in every facet of its operation. That volunteer spirit and the persistence that comes with ownership have seen the City survive every attack on its being and stability and will do so far into the future.

From Tectonic activity to mountains to shallow seas to earthquakes and volcanos. From Indian territories to European settlements to cattle ranches to a modern city. Fair Oaks Ranch has been a beacon on a hill. Fair Oaks Ranch is a story that needs to be told and remembered.

PART ONE

THE FOUNDATION

Every city in Texas is located in a county. Every county is part of the State. Every State is part of the country called The United States of America and part of the North American continent. The North American continent is in the western hemisphere. And that part of our globe we call earth had its beginning so long ago it defies true definition.

Still, what happened oh so long ago has a direct bearing on why we tend to love this part of Texas. *Part One – The Foundation* covers just a few of the past events that led up to the desirability of the area - a good place to live and raise a family.

The geology, flora and fauna, and culture of the area are strong magnets. How those came to be is an integral part of Fair Oaks Ranch as a city. The next few chapters cover only a portion of the vast amount of history and materials involved in the evolution of the area. Knowing where you've come from helps in knowing where you're going.

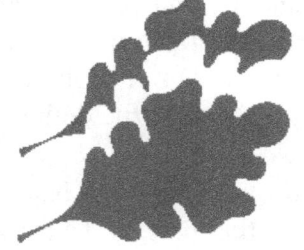

CHAPTER ONE - THE GEOLOGICAL BASE

Any Fair Oaks Ranch resident who has ever plunged a broad bladed shovel into the Hill Country ground in a vain attempt to find a space large enough to plant a tree has come face-to-face with the geology of this region. The thin, calcareous soils that overlay seemingly solid rock allow, at the most, only an inch or two of the shovel's blade to penetrate the surface before the rock beneath signals its total resistance. It is amazing that the soils that do find their way into the nooks and crannies of the rocks, like melting butter on an English Muffin, can support any form of plant species. But they do. And they do so in spades. Those rocks - certainly despised by a super-majority of

Chapter 1 History Of Fair Oaks Ranch

residents - demand the intrepid landscaper to take a pick when he goes afield rather than a shovel. And they are mere children from the geologist's viewpoint. It was the Miocene era that occurred only about 12 to 20 million years ago that created the conditions under which the Texas Hill Country and its foothills, including Fair Oaks Ranch, exist today. I'm certain many of us remember it well. And those hills are a thing of beauty and pride to anyone who is a Texan and calls Texas home. It is, in fact, the rocks that make the hills that provide the views that give us the character that fills us with pride for the land we love and cherish.

Although we may believe 12 to 20 million years is a long time, the more mature pre-Cambrian epoch of 1 billion or so years ago laid the foundation for everything else that came after. You can blame it all on the tectonic cycles of our globe that control the movement of the Earth's crust. It's pretty interesting so please don't hang your heads and moan. Mr. Tech Tonics did some rather major stuff to give us this land we love. And not just Texas, although that's most of what I'll talk about. He shaped our entire continent.

Anyway, it is probably safe to say that very few people within the City's confines think about how the City's physical countryside became what it is. The seemingly exorbitant amount of time for the geological processes to complete their missions can wear on the patience of a population that is on the go. In our persistent rush to get to the future we don't seem to have time to think about time. Strange. However, a brief understanding of what formed the beauty of the Hill Country and Fair Oaks Ranch is appropriate to this history.

History Of Fair Oaks Ranch — Chapter 1

We tend to look at rocks as solid, sometimes unmovable, objects (mostly unmovable when we find them with our shovels...uh...pick). In fact, they are somewhat liquid. Of course they take their good old time to move making the Ents from the popular trilogy *The Lord Of The Rings* seem to move at the speed of light. This all comes into focus if you accept the fact that the earth's crust is composed of a number of earthen plates that float atop a core of hot molten material like rubber ducks in a bathtub. The thin and relatively brittle crust made up of these plates and what we call our backyard is in constant motion over the more plastic substrata and provides the basis for tectonics.

By now it should be obvious that the study of the earth's plates and their movements and resulting deformation at the surface is known as tectonics.[1] Several tectonic cycles, called episodes by the experts, have affected Texas.[2] To the west and north of Fair Oaks Ranch Precambrian tectonic cycles were active in the Van Horn, El Paso, and Llano regions forming mountains that have literally gone under - younger rocks from subsequent eras have buried them deep in the earth's crust.[3]

By the time those cycles had ended, parts of the earth's crust in the area we now know as the State of Texas were moved a considerable distance and presently reside in places as far away as Antarctica and Australia.[4] This may be hard to believe, but the last I checked, Australians had a little of the Texas attitude and brashness in them. So it must be true.

Chapter 1   History Of Fair Oaks Ranch

Texas was again the target of tectonic violence, albeit at a very slow rate, during the Paleozoic Ouachitan Cycle. (Don't try to pronounce it. I did and ended up biting my tongue.) This period saw North and South America on a tectonic collision course about 550 million years ago. When the two continents finally met 300 million years after their long range planning sessions, their hell-bent for fury objectives resulted in the Ouachito Mountains – a vast range of rugged peaks that covered the southern and eastern central parts of Texas and even extended through an area way out east we now know as the Appalachian Mountain Range.[5]

Strange as it may seem with mountains growing like popcorn all around the place the tectonic clock moved forward slowly and eventually created places at the foot of the mountains much lower than the surrounding seas. It wasn't long (well, at least in tectonic terms) until much of Texas was inundated by the oceans. Shallow seas spread throughout the countryside where the mountainsides lost their ruggedness and sloped to the floor.[6]

Since even geological events seem to come in threes like disasters and other things of that venue, the current (and third) tectonic cycle known as the Gulf Coast cycle began with what is known as continental rifting or simply cracking and stretching into shallow basins. This activity created a situation in which the Earth's crust, once high and mighty, became the seabed under the Gulf of Mexico - sort of like your favorite T-shirt in the drawer after laundry day. This, combined with a companion mountain building event that formed the Rocky Mountains, was perhaps the strongest near-term event when considering the tectonic cycle's impact on Texas.

It seems the tectonic's most urgent activity is to build mountains. The most recent cycle is still in progress and the Gulf of Mexico and Rocky Mountain formations are part of a tectonic movement that is widening the Atlantic Ocean while simultaneously narrowing the Pacific Ocean.[7]

Having now gotten the most recent 50 plus million years of information out of the way we can talk about something closer to home and more readily understood and accepted by the more recent inhabitants. We witness in our daily travels many things evident from this history. But perhaps we don't recognize the significance of these abstract events on our lives in Fair Oaks Ranch. Some of what follows here is fodder for our love of the Hill Country. We just never think of it often.

If you ride anywhere along IH 35 between San Antonio and Austin you will notice flat, relatively uninteresting lands to the east of your travels. And, as though IH 35 was a line drawn in the rocks, you will see bumpy lands to the west. This is present day visual evidence of tectonic activity. To the west is an area called the Balcones Escarpment. To the east is the downward side of the Balcones fault which gave rise (no pun intended) to the escarpment to the west. This fault runs roughly from the northeast to the southwest from somewhere near Austin to somewhere south and west of San Antonio. It was formed about 12 to 25 million years ago – only yesterday in geological terms.[8] Right?

The rolling vistas we see today in the Texas Hill Country west

Chapter 1 — History Of Fair Oaks Ranch

of IH 35 and the flat expanses to the east of IH 35 are the direct result of an escarpment and ultimate erosion in its many forms on two types of rocks (Yes - rocks again. They will never go away). Those to the west are more resistant to erosion and have overcome the urge to become obliterated over time while those to the east have easily succumbed to the elements. An escarpment is generally the face of a dramatically uplifted plateau.[9] All of us who have lived here for some time are familiar with the Llano escarpment and other similar escarpments we see everywhere in the area and ooh and aah about all the time.

Our own personal escarpment is the Balcones and the uplifting to the west resulting from the activities of the fault is what we treasure as the Texas Hill Country. There are few who have not traveled within its hills and valleys and outcroppings who do not wonder at its beauty. Fair Oaks Ranch lies directly at the Hill Country's feet. The Balcones fault is, in fact, on our front porch. And we can once again blame, or is it now thank, tectonic activity for our good fortune.

Fair Oaks Ranch residents are very familiar with the erosion resistant rocks left over from all the tectonic cycles including the most recent sedimentary monstrosities that seem to always be right where you want to dig. They are our shovel's worst nightmares. Most of these rocks belong to a group known as Glen Rose limestone or Edwards limestone. Damn the rock if you will but the porous formations hundreds of feet beneath the surface are a godsend. The region is nearly totally dependent on the aquifer held in this stratum for its water supply. In fact, the millions of years of activity have given us a purity in our water that many have commercially exploited in plastic bottles.

Fortunately, all evidence indicates the Balcones fault is no longer in motion. At its most active time it moved as much as 700 feet over millions of years.[10] But not all at one time. Like most faults, movement is in spurts of a few feet every few hundred years – again a blink of an eye for the geologist. The closest to any Balcones movement we have now is the water flowing in the Balcones Creek which winds its way through part of the City before draining into the Cibolo Creek.

If it was possible to have a time lapsed photographic video of all these events it would certainly be fascinating. We would see high mountains perched on the present City of Austin and could watch both the movement of the landmass and the erosion of the mountains like slowly flowing molasses onto what is now the flat lands east of IH 35. The waters from the Gulf of Mexico once nestled at the foot of the mountains would be like children around the volunteer dad on a camping trip. These waters would slowly flood much of the area occupied once upon a time by mountains in the past and leave layer upon layer of Cretaceous deposits. We see these left overs in the strata exposed when the highway systems throughout the Hill Country cut into the understory of the rocky land. The shoreline of the Gulf of Mexico would move southward mainly because material eroded from the higher areas to the west would push it out to sea, so to speak. We would also see the rocks to the right of IH 35 stretching into their current thinness and slipping away from the Balcones fault after having probably caused the fault in the first place.

Chapter 1 History Of Fair Oaks Ranch

We would then see everything settle down for an extended siesta and await the arrival of man.[11]

As nature waited for the arrival of humans other changes would take place. Gone would be the Mississippi River that once flowed across East Texas. Gone would be the trans-Pecos volcanoes and the thick assault of lava flows. With the arrival of the relatively recent Ice Age the Pecos River would erode northward into New Mexico and the high plains would be carved up by several rivers. The Llano uplift's eastern edge would retreat westward to its present position. The rivers we know as the Colorado, the Brazos, the Red, and the Canadian would slowly become entrenched as gradual uplift occurred across Texas during the last million years and their relentless flow removed the softer rock. Sea level changes would first expose and then inundate the continental shelf and the geography of Texas, based on all of these factors, would become what we know today from the east near Louisiana to more than 600 miles to the west at New Mexico.[12]

The broad and changing environment is pleasantly at what seems to be a standstill because of its inordinately slow movement. What these major events left behind form the bedrock of one of the most successful cities in recent times. In a sense Fair Oaks Ranch is possible only because all of these events provided the environment that drew people to the area.

Like it or not. Find it interesting or boring. Believe it or don't. A billion years or so ago the area we call Fair Oaks Ranch was born.

CHAPTER TWO - THE ECOLOGICAL BASE

As mentioned in Chapter One, rocks are a major element of Fair Oaks Ranch life. Some residents see rocks as the only element of the City considering everybody has a host of them. And rocks are indeed a major facet of the landscape throughout the Hill Country. A short drive on some of our Hill Country roads will provide you with ample evidence of the surfeit of rocks in the many German built stone fences still in use more than 150 years after they were built. One of the better examples of these fences is only a few miles up Old #9 Road from its intersection with RR 473 east of Comfort. Yet, the fossils we find in those rocks give strong evidence that something else besides tectonics was critical to the formation of the area's history and important to the Fair Oaks Ranch we know today.

Once all the events of the Balcones Fault and the escarpment and the uplifting and all the other geological cycles had settled in for a little snooze, the more dynamic elements of flora and fauna had their time in the sun. The average resident of Fair Oaks Ranch may not be involved in plant and animal life to the detail that inspires awe, but nearly every resident who wants to grow something that flowers and is pretty becomes an expert on what does and doesn't work. The landscaper is also quite familiar with the animals and soils that challenge the success of any outdoor effort. Anyone living in Fair Oaks Ranch can attest to that if only because of the deer.

Flora and fauna during the Pleistocene era are fairly well known but the vegetative history over the last 22,000 years is pretty sketchy.[1] Oil deposits below us (even in southern Bexar county)[2] are testament to vast quantities and varieties of plant life in this area before everything got buried under an avalanche of the tectonic variety. It was, as you can imagine, a less than habitable time. The current Eagle Ford shale operation south of Bexar County is a part of that history as well.

Life in the Hill Country wasn't any better for the first humans who showed up about 11,000 years ago. And when they did wander into the area near Fair Oaks Ranch they mostly shied away from the Hill Country in favor of the land to the east. But farming was possible if you worked at it. Few did. As a result the native plants and animals had relative freedom to grow, multiply, roam, and live with little interference. And they did just that.

For purposes of what's important to Fair Oaks Ranch, however, we need go back only into the sixteenth century and trace the use and misuse of the plants, lands, and animals that resulted in the environment we all seem to love and want to now protect.

If you spend any time looking at the land to your left and right during a trip through the Hill Country you can easily draw a conclusion that there are only a few plants that can survive our drought stricken, torridly hot summers. With an average rainfall measured in inches in the upper twenties to the mid-thirties (one source works it out as 36 inches)[3] we are on the tipping edge of becoming a semi-desert. And with much of that rain coming in spurts mostly in May and September, we suffer long periods of very unfriendly conditions. Yet, all the native plants have adapted over the years to these challenges and take the extremes in stride, even during the worst drought on record in 2011 and second worst drought and the driest single year on record during 2007 - 2009.[4]

What may not be apparent is that the Edwards Plateau (and, by association, the Hill Country) is an extension of the Great Plains. The Plateau grades gradually into the Rolling Plains of the country's midsection on its northward edges.[5] Much of the Edwards Plateau in the north is undissected and is indebted to the grasslands of the Great Plains for its topography and plant life.[6] Similar conditions existed in the Hill Country before it

Chapter 2 — History Of Fair Oaks Ranch

became hilly. But, as we now know, with the arrival of the tectonic cycles everything changed.

The erosion that followed the uplift created steep canyons and secluded valleys with a mixture of soil conditions. And along the Balcones Escarpment there arose a complex variety of plant life influenced by the Gulf Coastal Plain and the Edwards Plateau in juxtaposition. The Blackland Prairies even get a foothold in this area as a finger of its presence stretches in a narrow strip all the way down through the center of Bexar County.[7] This variety of soil types creates interesting challenges for anyone wishing to grow landscaping plants for recreation. In my own yard I have three types of soil. It's like fishing in muddy water; you never know what you're getting until you get it in the wheelbarrow.

Throughout our area we still find a great variety of microsystems. The rugged hillsides host plants that have adapted to the nearly absent soil conditions they endure while the streamside riparian habitats support water hungry trees such as the Bald Cypress which once supported a thriving roofing shingle industry in Bandera, Texas.[8]

It may seem that the variety that once covered the area has gone the way of the prairie. Everywhere you look you see Ash Juniper or 'Cedar', as the locals call it, and Live Oak, Red Oaks, Hackberry and maybe a few other trees. The flowers seem limited to Bluebonnets and Indian Blankets and a few others like Mexican Hats and a variety of yellow daisies. But variety does live on. For example, the book Wildflowers of the Texas Hill Country lists over 75 families and has a twelve page index of only a few of the flowers actively growing.[9] Also, the book Trees, Shrubs, and Vines of the Texas Hill Country by Jan Wrede, a one-time resident of Fair Oaks Ranch, discusses more than 120 species of the more common plants in this woody class.[10] On a personal note, I have observed over 250 species of plants and trees on my own little plot of land here in the City.

The only thing that has changed dramatically from historical perspectives is that which makes us want to live here - The Hill Country showed up. Of course we changed that significantly over the last 100 years. What once was a land of grasses is now mostly wooded land. Heavy grazing on the ridges of the hills, the only places where grasses could really get a foothold, had a major effect on the soil depth and texture.[7] Also, the 'Cedar' was not always as prevalent but has now created thick groves called 'cedar breaks' where grasses once thrived.

What all this means to the residents of Fair Oaks Ranch may not be apparent on first blush. But the sequence of tectonic activity followed by plant life in all its forms has created what we call the beauty of the Hill Country and is a prime factor in influencing the migration into what would be an otherwise inhospitable region.

Back to the 1700s for a minute, however. When the first settlers, other than the Indians, ventured into this area, the soil was already thin from millennia of erosion. But it was certainly a little better than now because it had yet to be trammeled by a hundred years of sheep, goats, and cattle. And this competition for scarce resources had an impact on the wildlife as well.

The result of the misuse of the land in the Blackland Prairie and the Hill Country was significant. By the end of the nineteenth century, the soils in the Prairie that were once the richest in the nation, required heavy fertilization to produce an acceptable crop. Overgrazing by cattle, sheep, and goats in the Hill Country had depleted the available forbs, the white-tailed deer's primary source of food. With the forbs depleted the deer population was reduced so badly they were rarely seen.[11]

Gone also are the herds of Bison that once roamed throughout the region. Bone beds in Val Verde County contain Bison remains from Indian pursuits where they drove the animals off cliffs and killed them for food, clothing and other uses. Other areas have camel, horse, and antelope remains. Even evidence of elephants can be found in Uvalde and northern Bexar Counties.[12] It's hard to believe deer were so rare back then when we experience the severe overpopulation evident every day in our yards and along our streets.

Nature can be amazingly adaptive and the native plants and animals knew how to fend off drought followed by flood. They have developed extensive defenses against the elements and now abound with the help of concerned citizens in organizations like the Native Plant Society of Texas and property owners who are committed to improving an already beautiful area.

You may love or hate the deer, raccoon, armadillo, fox, and

other persistent wildlife in the area. You may be frustrated or indifferent about the drought-flood cycles we experience seemingly on an annual basis. You may love or hate the rocky soils and the effort it takes to grow anything. But it is the combination of the geographical basis and the flora and fauna of the ecological basis that created the atmosphere that made the Hill Country a popular place to live and which beckons us to stay.

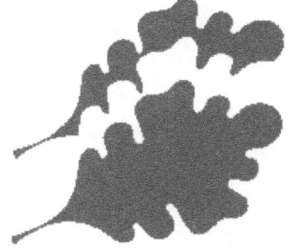

CHAPTER 3 – THE ANTHROPOLOGICAL BASE

The third facet of the City's magnetism lies in the culture bred in the locals for more than 150 years. That culture is ingrained in the City itself now and is discussed throughout the remainder of this book. But how it all came to be is a most interesting story. The history books are replete with almost unlimited detail about Texas and the Hill Country culture and its inhabitants and their immigration into the area. This chapter will not try to cover all the detail or include every nuance of the changes over the centuries. Only an overview is possible at this time.

Chapter 3   History Of Fair Oaks Ranch

The first evidence of human activity in this area that the anthropologists can uncover indicates our species has lived here for only a mere 11,000 years.[1] During this prehistoric era there were three major periods of human activity that shaped the population of the Hill Country prior to the arrival of Europeans. These periods are called the Paleo-Indian, Archaic, and the Late Prehistoric.[2]

Little is known about the Paleo-Indian period but evidence indicates that during its lengthy period, made up of three distinct segments, humans were primarily hunter gatherers. Some of this evidence is located in Northern Bexar County along the Salado Creek which, incidentally, has its headwaters in Fair Oaks Ranch near the Norman Vestal Homeowners Park including a seep spring in my backyard. There is evidence of Bison hunting in certain areas and the existence of cemeteries indicates that there was a growing sense of territoriality.[3]

Things really picked up steam during the Prehistoric period which began about 800 A.D. and ended with the European immigration. The bow and arrow were developed and replaced spear throwing as a means of obtaining food. Bison population peaked around 1200 A.D. and ranged as far south as Alice, Texas. Much of this evidence comes from caves in the area that were used by the people for shelter and as homes.[4]

The Spanish were the first immigrants to view and explore what is now Texas in 1519. They settled here shortly after that and remained a force for over 300 years contributing a significant amount of culture and history. In fact, the Spanish explorers and conquistadors were roaming across the area long before the English settled the Atlantic coast.[5] Their longest uninterrupted period of control, however, lasted only 105 years from 1716 until 1821. Yet the plethora of Spanish names for towns and geographic landmarks throughout Texas is evidence of the power they once held. It was during this time that San Antonio was established as the first formal municipality in an area that was to eventually become Texas.[6]

The Spanish migration into the area was like one of our famous warm fronts as the immigrants traveled up from the Gulf Coast. But eventually many more found their way into the territory from New Mexico and Louisiana to the west and east.[7] Spain had acquired Louisiana from the French when the latter ceded it to them as a consequence of the French and Indian wars. This territory included all the French held lands west of the Mississippi. But, as the period history shows, Spain was also unable to defend the vast territory and eventually invited the English into the area to settle it.[8]

In an attempt to maintain control over the area Spain's King Charles III ordered an inspection of the territory, thought of at the time as part of the Spanish Empire. Even with the help of the English settlers the efforts to maintain control failed and Spain had to retrocede the lands back to the French in 1800.[9] The struggle for Mexican independence, begun in 1810, spelled the final failure of Spain's dominance in the region, not the least spurred on by the United States' purchase of the Louisiana Territory in 1803[10] and the growing sense of independence prevalent throughout Texas.

Chapter 3   History Of Fair Oaks Ranch

You may recall the Balcones Escarpment, mentioned in Chapter One, as the major geological feature of the area. It also became a major cultural factor in the years to come. Central Texas was virtually unsettled until well into the 18th century. The earliest Spanish settlement was the Mission San Antonio de Valero known now as The Alamo.[11] The road connecting this mission to areas both east and west was known as the Camino Real and followed the escarpment mentioned earlier. Remnants of this royal road still exist. A good portion of it follows State Highway 21 from New Braunfels to Bryan/College Station.

The land west of the escarpment remained relatively free of European settlement even up to the 1840s.[12] But in 1821 Moses Austin established a colony north of San Antonio that opened that area to development and by 1830 English speaking whites outnumbered Mexicans by a factor of 3 to 1.[13]

Comanche and Apache Indians were relative newcomers to the Hill Country but they and lesser bands of Indians were predominant mostly in the lands to the west of the escarpment well into the 1840s. The Indians, native to the area around Fair Oaks Ranch, were the Tonkawa and the Coahuiltecan. They were a more peaceful people but were forced out of the Hill Country by the more aggressive Comanche who had migrated down the country from the northwest and raided the local area frequently.[14]

It is the German migration into the area, however, that had the most influence on our lives here. The founding of New Braunfels in 1844 set the stage for large scale German immigration.[15] But it was not without consequence as the experiences of immigrants who traveled from Indianola to New Braunfels in the 1870s tells us. Six thousand immigrants had unloaded in this coastal community and worked their way to the New City up north. By the time they arrived only 1,500 remained.[16] Other immigration catastrophes included the loss of an entire ship's population to yellow fever.[17] In spite of these terrible hardships the immigrations continued unabated until a sizeable population existed throughout the region.

By 1845 Texas was finally admitted to the Union and by the end of the Civil War, during which the last conflict of the war occurred at the Battle of Palmito Ranch in Texas, there were more than 40,000 head of cattle and sheep in the Boerne area alone.[18] But the German population was also growing. There were 250 to 300 German settlements in the area. Comal County had 3,627 Germans and only 94 Anglo-Americans.[19] Between 1844 and 1847 alone more than 7,000 Germans arrived in the area.

These large numbers resulted in German speaking settlements and a strong German cultural influence in the area that persists in many places to this day. These characteristics include an independent character, religious faith, conservative thinking and other self-reliant attitudes.

In the late 1840s, Germans escaping the revolutions in Germany came to an area on the Cibolo Creek and established a camp they called Tuscalum near present day Johns Road in Boerne, Texas. The camp was eventually platted as a city in 1851 and named after Ludwig Borne who had encouraged many to migrate to the new world.[20]

"Free Thinkers" – Germans who had no religion – controlled the City at that time. George Wilkins Kendall, for whom the County is named, requested permission to build a church to honor his wife in the City. But the atheistic Free Thinkers denied him approval. As a result, he built his church south of the town just outside the City limits.[21] You can still see that church, known as St. Peter's Catholic Church as you drive by West Kronkosky Street on South Main Street. There was a recent controversy over this same church when a recently established Historical Society successfully fought to prohibit the removal of the building. More than one hundred fifty years ago, no one wanted the church in the city and now no one wants it taken away. Time changes all things.

A century and a half later we are still influenced by much of the German culture. The immigrants were educators, craftsmen, musicians, physicians, lawyers, teachers, journalists, authors, and many other professionals. They brought with them European-style stone architecture, brass bands, schools and libraries, and choral societies. In fact, for many years there were more German language newspapers than English. Only in 1957 did the last German language newspaper cease publication.[22]

Texas, from the Caddo Indian word Tejas, means friend.[23] Many of us have come to this area because of its friendliness. But much more than that we have been drawn to the area by its geography, ecology, and culture. These three aspects of living in the Hill Country are major aspects of anyone's decision to live in Fair Oaks Ranch. Still the 1800s were a long time ago. What has happened since then? What changes have taken place? How did this city come to be and become what it is today? What makes Fair Oaks Ranch unique among cities in Texas and why does it matter?

That is the subject of the next part of this book.

Chapter 3 — History Of Fair Oaks Ranch

PART TWO

THE FORMATION

When the founding fathers began their efforts to create a city made up of a bedroom development known as Fair Oaks Ranch, they had no idea how to do it or what challenges they would face in the process. But they shared a vision of what the new city should look like and how it should function.

It took a concerted attack on bureaucracy by many individuals and the support of the entire community to make it happen. It took the desires of the residents for autonomy to get it going. It took an unprecedented commitment and trust between the developer and the new city to get it born and to survive its early years. It took the spirit of freedom from an absent landlord known as San Antonio to get it all together.

Part Two – The Formation is what it advertises by its name: the formation of the city with all its warts and weaknesses. But the approach was one of common sense and faith in the promises of the developer. It all came true and turned out to be historic. But before the history could be told, the beginning had to happen.

CHAPTER FOUR - COMMON SENSE GOVERNMENT

The City of Fair Oaks Ranch would never have found birth without two major events that occurred during the Twentieth Century. The first of these two events was when a young Romanian boy of fourteen decided to run away from home. He quickly found work in the oil industry and began a career that would become legendary.

This boy was Ralph Fair, Sr. and his lifelong career in the oil industry saw him achieve a level of success few people of his generation had known. He travelled extensively as part of his job and his involvement with Pop Joyner, who discovered the East Texas oil fields, was a major influence on him. During his young adult life he worked on the development of the Ploiesti

Chapter 4 — History Of Fair Oaks Ranch

Oil Fields in Romania, a place that later became a major source of oil for Nazi Germany.

All of these activities allowed him to amass enough wealth to  begin purchasing large tracts of property in Kendall, Comal, and Bexar Counties south of Boerne, Texas, in the 1930s. At the time, he had no idea or plans for the land becoming one of the most successful cities in the country. His only goal was to create a ranch where he could pursue his ranching activities and his hobbies.

He came to the area looking for contiguous parcels of land suitable for ranching. Eventually, and with the help of his brother-in-law, Bill Phelp, he assembled 7 to 10 such parcels and bought them from the various owners who had title at the time.[1] Although the ranch finally encompassed 5,000 acres, the original area of the ranch was only that portion north of Dietz Elkhorn Road. Ralph Fair, Sr., later purchased the land south of this road to add to his holdings after he had moved to the ranch.[1]

Ralph Fair's ranching activities had to continue without his presence during World War II as he, like millions of others in the country, answered the call to serve. He worked under General William 'Wild Bill' Donovan in the Office of Strategic Services while his first son Wallace was the General's aide.[1] But it was his intimate knowledge of the Ploiesti oil field facilities that proved to be his most valuable contribution to the Allies. He assisted in the plan for their destruction during World War II. As part of the effort he helped construct mockups of the oil field facilities in the African desert so pilots could practice recognizing and hitting their targets.[2] All the while back home in Texas his wife, Dorothy, managed the ranch, raised chickens, and sold eggs at the ranch unaware he was destroying what he had built years before.

Prior to the war, Ralph Fair, Sr., was an active race horse enthusiast. When Texas law changed and prohibited gambling on horses in 1937 he was forced into another line of activity on the ranch. In response, he transitioned to cattle ranching and established wide spread credentials in breeding Polled Herefords, the red and white cows seen frequently throughout the country. His most famous bull, Battle Intense, gained notoriety when he became involved in an artificial insemination program rarely used at the time.[3]

Battle Intense's fame was unexpected, however, for in the beginning the more expensive bull, known as Larry Domino, was purchased to spearhead this program. Unfortunately, Larry Domino's calves didn't turn out so well. Try after try resulted in inferior calves, dwarfs of no value to cattle ranchers or the cattle industry as a whole.[1] As a result, Battle Intense inherited the title role of inseminator in the new reproduction program and went on to become a very valuable and honored animal. He lives on in memory now with an annual golfing tournament named for him at the Country Club on the ranch.

Following the deaths of Ralph Fair, Sr., and his wife Dorothy

Chapter 4 — History Of Fair Oaks Ranch

in the 1967 and 1969 respectively, Ralph Fair, Jr., and his two half sisters, Doris and Isabel, and half-brother, Wallace, tried to continue managing the cattle along with a dairy operation and hunting leases. Try as they might and even after long hours and hard work they soon realized that the cattle operation in the early 1970s was a losing proposition. Expenses far outpaced income and, if allowed to continue, would soon deplete sustainable resources. Even the dairy business, which was the only profitable operation on the ranch, was not sufficient to allay the financial hemorrhage. After much thought and discussion the family finally made the difficult decision to sell the ranch.

Economic conditions in the early 1970s were not conducive to marketing such a large property and these sales efforts also failed. Nobody seemed interested in such a large piece of property. It seemed as though everything was on a slippery slope toward disaster. But it was their inability to find a buyer for the ranch that became the second most important event in the formation of the City of Fair Oaks Ranch.

Looking back on that failure it is now quite apparent that the area was fortunate that there were no buyers for the land. Had the sales effort succeeded there would most likely be no City of Fair Oaks Ranch. Most probably a plethora of suburban developments of differing cultures such as are currently populating what is left of the country between San Antonio and the City would have pre-empted any city formation effort. It was at this time that all four of the heirs made the critical decision that set in motion activities resulting ultimately in what is now a thriving and beautiful city in great demand. The heirs agreed to develop the property and set about making that project more successful than either their ranching or their sales efforts could ever have been.

Ralph Fair, Jr., having been appointed by the heirs as the sole authority for managing the development, approached Don Smith, a developer responsible for the Trailwood and Windwood developments on the west side of IH 10. At first, Don declined to become involved as he had commitments to clients in Windwood that he would have to break should he accept the offer. However, with the persistent encouragement of Ralph Fair, Jr., he later was able to clear the way to participate and he joined the Ralph Fair Incorporation team, remaining with it for more than 35 years.

Many in the industry believed the ranch was too distant from San Antonio to be a successful development. The target market included professionals such as doctors and executives who commuted to their work places in San Antonio. The prevailing thought was that no one would want to drive that far just to have a home in the country. To them it seemed like an absurd idea. In spite of these professional concerns, the developers were convinced of the marketability of the property and proceeded with the first section containing large 10 to 20 acre mini-ranches on the north part of the ranch.

The first sales office was located in a building near the old dairy barn at the intersection of Ralph Fair Road (called Curry Creek Road at the time) and Dietz Elkhorn Road.[5] This building would eventually become the second of three locations for the City offices and eventually the police force headquarters. The complex also included a small cabin that was occupied at the time by Eddie Strelzik, an employee of

Chapter 4   History Of Fair Oaks Ranch

the ranch whose duties in this 'remote' area included providing security and pursuing poachers. This cabin is now the location of the City's Community Center which also houses the Fair Oaks Ranch Homeowners Association (FORHA). The dairy barn nearby housed the dairy operation using Holsteins and Jerseys[1] and is now part of the City's maintenance and utilities operation.

All that was needed at the time to sell these unimproved lots was an aerial photograph of the land with some lines drawn on it showing the general layout of the property in question. No fancy plats or metes and bounds documents were required and there were no roads constructed. To properly view the land, a jeep or other all-terrain vehicle was needed. By all standards that are now in place with GPS, Google Maps, satellite views and such, the approach was pretty rugged and ragged.

The only access to this northern portion of the ranch was up Curry Creek Road. A short portion of that road still holding the same name is Old Curry Creek Road near Bergheim. The name most current residents are familiar with is Ralph Fair Road or FM 3351, now a major artery to IH 10 and San Antonio to the south and all points north and east of Boerne. The entrance to the main ranch complex including Ralph Fair, Sr.'s, home was at what is now west of the intersection of Dietz Elkhorn Road and No Le Hace at 7595 Dietz Elkhorn where the rock columns with a connecting lodge pole still stand. The original plots required owners to drill their own wells and install septic systems. The roads were installed without curbs and with bar ditches along the sides to maintain its country atmosphere.[4]

By all modern measurements of business activity, the development should not have succeeded. It was a good ways outside San Antonio. There were few services. You had to drill your own well and install a septic system. There were no amenities - just country atmosphere. You bought the land and you had to do something with it yourself or you just owned a large piece of dirt.

But a significant element contributing to the development's success was the business model Ralph Fair, Jr., insisted on employing. Unheard of at the time and possibly still rare, if not extinct, was his policy of returning the buyer's investment any time the buyer felt the purchase had been a mistake. No questions asked. No reason needed. This simple commitment, combined with the positive reputation that Ralph Fair, Sr., had built in the region, was very effective. And when combined with Ralph Fair, Jr.'s, commitment to providing value in return for investment it resulted in the parcels selling rapidly. In fact, as if to ridicule the naysayers, there were a number of bidders per parcel each seeking the right to buy. In short order, all the lots were sold.[5]

Don Smith relates how they had so many buyers for each parcel that they put all the names in a box, shook it around, and pulled a name out of the box much as choosing a door prize winner. The bearer of the name retrieved in this manner had the first rights of purchase. And the naysayers shook their

Chapter 4 — History Of Fair Oaks Ranch

heads in amazement. A fluke. It won't last. Surprise.

Following this success, Don Smith thought smaller parcels in the south portion of the ranch would also work. However, the Interstate Land Sales Act created an impediment to the development of these smaller tracts south of the Cibolo Creek. Under the Act, the parcels in the development had to be registered with the authorities in Washington, D.C. and approval granted before any action could be taken. The rapid sales of the north lots provided the confidence needed to develop smaller 2 to 5 acre lots but without getting the authority under the Act no one could move forward.

The normal process of application for approval and waiting for said approval was as frustrating back then as it is now. In spite of the appropriate documents having been submitted, the application to conform with the Act was stonewalled in Washington, D.C. and the development of the smaller plots was stymied. "Somehow, somewhere, someone applied some much needed pressure with the authorities," Don Smith related to me during an interview. "And – ahoy – approval was finally granted."

And the boys to the south waited in the wings to gloat when their predictions of failure would certainly come true.

With approval in hand, Don Smith quickly designed the smaller lots. Because of their size, however, a significant problem arose - how to provide sufficient water to each lot. They didn't want to require the landowners to drill their own wells on such small lots. Such a requirement would add significantly to the costs of ownership and the marketability of the properties. It would also create an area of nearly unrestricted and uncontrolled drinking straws driven into the Trinity Aquifer system.

As a result, what is now the City water system was born as Glenpool, Inc.. From that point forward all lots developed had water supplied through this underground distribution system. And true to Ralph Fair Jr.'s, commitment to value, the water was provided free to the residents during the first two years of their ownership of the land.[4]

It didn't take long for one of the first upscale homes to be built on these new sized lots. In 1977 a house was built on a five acre parcel and nicknamed 'the Enchanted House that speaks for itself' due, in part, to its full house electronic intercom system. At the time it was one of the most innovative and technologically inspired homes on the ranch and a first of its kind in the greater San Antonio area. Marketed as Das Landhaus (The Country Home) it set a standard for homes that followed in its wake and continues to this day.

Things were rolling on the ranch and business was demanding a lot out of the few employees of Ralph E. Fair, Inc. So in 1977, Ralph Fair, Jr., made what could be the most significant decision related to the success of both the development and the formation of the City. He hired a young civil engineer from Denver working in the petroleum industry to manage the family's oil and gas interests. That young man was Robert Weiss (or Bob as we all came to know him) and his duties quickly expanded until he became the senior official representing Ralph Fair, Jr., Ralph E. Fair, Inc. and the developers.

Chapter 4 — History Of Fair Oaks Ranch

Robert Weiss' efforts and cooperative approach over the next 35 years were the single most important aspect of the City becoming what it is today. That is not to say the founding fathers were not incredibly valuable. Without them there would be no City. But without the influence and team attitude Bob Weiss brought to the table and the unwavering support of Ralph Fair, Jr., the City's growth and quality would have suffered and possibly fallen into disrepair. His contributions are often overlooked but not lessened by time. As Bob told me: "Ralph Fair asked me to help manage his oil and gas interests. When I got here he told me 'Oh. By the way. There's something else I'd like you to do'." We are lucky he did that something else.

As part of the planned development with Bob Weiss managing the business operations and Don Smith handling the sales aspects, they insisted that there be a Homeowners Association from the very beginning.[5] The requirement evolved naturally as it was in direct support of Ralph Fair Jr.'s commitment to value. The Homeowners Association's duties included the preparation and enforcement of restrictions on the use of the land. And as each new section was developed, the restrictions for that section were to be tailored to that section's unique needs. It was this act of insisting on a Homeowners Association that ultimately paved the way for the formation of a city.

As the development continued with the smaller lots, Don Smith suggested they develop a golf course to help with the viability of the community. After all, wasn't the target market doctors and lawyers and executives? Although there was little enthusiasm for the effort, Don Smith and Bob Weiss met with the owners of the limestone pit that is now known as The Rim Shopping Center. They gave the owners an offer to become partners in the proposed golf course operation they had planned. The response was immediate and unfavorable. The logic followed the same pattern of the naysayers of old who still didn't understand what was evolving north of San Antonio. There was a development in the Bandera area that was failing at that time and the gravel pit's owners were not yet convinced that the Fair Oaks Ranch development would succeed in spite of the on-going successful sales of property. As a result of this denial, Ralph Fair, Jr., once again agreed to proceed on his own.

If you want a golf course you need to hire someone who knows about golf to design it. After working with numerous candidates, Gary Player, a South African golfer who had won 24 Professional Golf Association Tour competitions by April 1978, was promptly enlisted to design the course.[5] Before settling on Gary Player, previous candidates had

insisted that a new and modern club house needed to be constructed as part of the golf course design. The thinking was that the old Fair home (now the club house) was not suitable and would inhibit the course's profitability. It is thus interesting to learn that when Gary Player arrived on the scene

Chapter 4 — History Of Fair Oaks Ranch

to discuss the golf course he asked a simple question that had amazing repercussions.

"What do you intend to do with the house?" he asked.[5]

The resulting discussion ended in the Fair home becoming the club house. It became a great club house and remains so to this day with improvements and expansions that have served the community more than was initially envisioned.

As the development grew in the area south of Dietz Elkhorn Road it became apparent that an easier access to IH 10 was required. The Ralph Fair Road route was not conducive to the volume of traffic expected nor the timeliness of transit. Fortunately, the Pfieffer family, who owned the land between the ranch and IH 10 at the time, serendipitously approached Don Smith with the idea of developing some of their land as part of the Fair Oaks Ranch activity. Little did anyone know how prescient this thought would become. As a result of this contact, they were able to extend Fair Oaks Parkway through the Pfieffer land and gain direct access to IH 10 at the overpass that crossed into the Windwood and Trailwood developments.[5]

Progress was about to become unpreventable. The naysayers were about to be silenced. The large lots in the north were sold out. The smaller lots in the south were selling like hotcakes even though they were 'too far from San Antonio'. The properties were now easily accessible from IH 10. The Ralph E. Fair, Inc. organization's commitment to quality was entrenched. The Fair Oaks Ranch development had become a community.

From that point forward there was no turning back and over the next 35 years the community grew without hesitation or hiccup. What was once an area of less than a dozen or so residents became an incorporated city of more than 6,000 people with still more growth in the future. Once a ranch of 5,000 acres it is now a city of more than 8,000 acres and the demand to live here remains strong. How all that came about is a most interesting and noble story.

Chapter 4

CHAPTER FIVE – VISIONARY THINKING WINS

On October 31, 1931, Erwin Louis and Rosa Lee Gaubatz became the proud parents of a son. They named him Erwin Louis Gaubatz, Jr. He was like any other boy born in that time in San Antonio, Texas, except that he loved to wear his father's cowboy boots. As a youngster the boots travelled up his legs to his hips and made him look like he had no legs at all – just long ankles and big feet. With the boots as his constant companions, he eventually earned a nickname that would stay with him throughout his entire life.[1] "Boots" became a moniker that in nearly all instances replaced his given name and became the method of address he preferred. The nickname would also become synonymous with the vision he created that was bold in scope and daunting in application. "Boots" Gaubatz made his parents proud as a child but they could never have imagined how proud he would have made them if they could have witnessed what he accomplished in Fair Oaks Ranch. His vision of a community free from outside interference or control became reality on his watch and Fair Oaks Ranch and Boots Gaubatz eventually became pretty near synonymous as well.

Boots attended Thomas Jefferson High School in San Antonio, Texas, and graduated in 1949. His stint as President of the Student Council and training as a U.S. Air Force officer gave him valuable skills he would later use as he worked for Southwestern Bell Telephone Company as well as when he entered the political arena. He married June Meredith Durst in 1957 and together, as he climbed the executive ladder of a successful career, they moved their family 17 times in 20 years through 11 cities in Texas, Missouri, Kansas, Arkansas, and Washington, D.C.

He returned to San Antonio in 1980 where he was the General Manager of Network Distribution Services for Southwestern Bell Telephone Company. On his arrival he and his family moved to a community northwest of San Antonio known as Fair Oaks Ranch where he immediately became involved in community affairs. He soon earned the volunteer position of President of the Fair Oaks Ranch Homeowners Association that Ralph Fair, Jr. had insisted on establishing at the beginning of the development. His presidency would soon become pivotal to the formation of the City.

When he and his family moved to Fair Oaks, the development

was still in its relative infancy. Most of the 5,000 acre ranch had yet to be platted and the homes that were built were scattered throughout the limited developed portions. Although most of the platted properties were sold, many were still vacant and the area had a country feel that drew the interest of a growing number of buyers. But all of that was to change within mere weeks of Boots' arrival.

In the early 1980s and before Boots had moved to the ranch, a procurement scandal in the U.S. Air Force led to a Congressional response in the form of the Competition In Contracting Act (CICA). This Act established an organization at Kelly Air Force Base charged with overseeing the procurement process and expanding competition for government contracts. A young man by the name of David Deleranko was assigned to that organization and his association with the staff of the City of San Antonio would become one of the most important relationships in securing Fair Oaks Ranch's autonomy.[2]

David owned property in Fair Oaks Ranch but had not yet built a home. However, he was planning to settle there as soon as finances and detailed construction planning allowed. He considered his efforts at clearing the land and building infrastructure an investment and he intended to protect it. Therefore, a conversation he had with a San Antonio staffer in early 1986 evoked strong feelings that all his hard work on the property, his investment, would be diminished.[2]

The staffer informed him that San Antonio was planning a 'Finger Annexation' along Interstate Highway 10 as far as Boerne, Texas. This annexation would effectively place an area within a five mile radius from the point on the highway they chose for the city limits under the control of San Antonio and subject to all the City authority including eventual taxation.[2]

Extra-territorial jurisdiction is the term for this authority. It is a geographical and political term that roughly translates to 'we own you but we don't want you living in our house. When we decide to include you, you will have to move in whether you like it or not.' The Fair Oaks Ranch vision did not allow for San Antonio to tell the community what to do. It did not fit with the will of the residents. It wasn't our desire. It was also a serious challenge to what David had planned for his homestead.

He began researching incorporation law and obtained a template for incorporation from a small community called Oak Village North, now located in Bulverde, Texas. Armed with San Antonio's unpublished plans, his research in incorporation law, and the template, he approached The President of the Fair Oaks Ranch Homeowners Association - E. L. "Boots" Gaubatz.[2]

As a result of this new information and in light of the significant effect it would have on Fair Oaks Ranch, Boots called an emergency meeting of the FORHA officers in May 1986 wherein they discussed alternatives and how to respond to the threat. The outcome of the meeting was the formation of an Incorporation Committee headed by Don King, the Association's Director of Planning at that time.

Through a stroke of good fortune in the FORHA meeting

when this committee was formed, a new resident was in attendance. Typical of Boots' demeanor he introduced himself and learned a little about Brigadier General Robert Herring. Born in 1921 in Lawrence County, Mississippi, General Herring was the son of a country school teacher who entered the ministry while General Herring was still a young boy. After graduating from high school in 1939, he attended Clark College and Harding University in Mississippi and Southwest Baptist Theological Seminary. With his Masters of Divinity and Theology in hand, he joined the U. S. Army as a Chaplain and worked his way up the ranks to the grade of brigadier general - an accomplishment almost never heard of in the Chaplain career field.

Boots did not delay long in asking the general to serve on the Homeowners Association Board of Directors and participate in a committee looking at the future of the FORHA and its organization. General Herring graciously accepted the invitation. The Association held its annual meetings in November each year and when General Herring attended his first annual meeting as a board member that fall in 1986, he was elected to serve as the Association's President, replacing Boots in that capacity. In this position, he was pivotal to the success of efforts to escape San Antonio's grasp less than a month later.[3]

Things and events were on a fast track during the spring, summer, and fall of 1986 as the Incorporation Committee, sometimes referred to as the Committee of Ten, worked diligently to organize the effort to incorporate the community. Time was of the essence if they were to achieve their goal of becoming a city before San Antonio was able to advance its

ETJ up IH 10 and therefore prevent the desired Fair Oaks Ranch incorporation from happening.

The Committee of Ten recommended that the original 5,000 acres of Fair Oaks Ranch be incorporated as soon as possible. However, there was a serious obstacle to this action in the Texas Local Government code. There were certain population and territorial requirements for incorporation as a general-law municipality. This law specifically states that a community with fewer than 2,000 inhabitants (which applied to Fair Oaks Ranch development at the time) must not have more than 2 square miles of surface area. Inasmuch as 5000 acres equals 7.8125 square miles the entire ranch exceeded these limitations.[4]

The only workable solution was to create two cities each being less than 2 square miles. The boundaries of each of these cities would be constructed in such a fashion that they encompassed the outer perimeter of the Ranch and connected with each other at the sides thus isolating the interior of the development and preventing San Antonio access. This structure would also allow one of the two cities to annex the other at a later date - the plan from the very beginning. The FORHA attorney, Harvey Hardy, supported this approach and verified its legality. As a result, the committee prepared maps and plans with hopes that the Association's membership would also support the approach.

The unique aspects of this approach have never been given their due regards. Without the forward thinking of the committee that developed this approach, Fair Oaks Ranch would never have become anything other than a bedroom community of San Antonio. It would never have become the entity and the envy of others it has become. And it would have eventually been annexed by either Boerne or San Antonio with all the big city bureaucracy that comes with annexation.

The FORHA held numerous Town Hall Meetings at various locations such as the Sons of Hermann Hall on Dietz Elkhorn Road, the local country club, and the fire station at the entrance to the Raintree Wood entrance which were the only locations in the City large enough to hold more than a small group of people. Boots Gaubatz, Don King, Robert Herring, and others involved with the Committee of Ten campaigned in support of the City formation at these meetings.

A key element in what was proposed was that of trust. There was no way in which either of the cities could be forced into annexation with the other. Also, by forming a boundary around the ranch, the unincorporated portions were protected from annexation by not only an outside municipality but both of the newly formed cities as well. The lack of contiguousness created an island within the new cities that was under no obligation to request annexation by any city or government authority. It was a unique and fragile arrangement.

No matter how it all turned out, trust was trump. Since the vast majority of the undeveloped land within the circle of protection built by the committee still belonged to Ralph E. Fair, Inc., the homeowners would have to trust Ralph Fair, Jr., and his key development manager, Bob Weiss, to do the right thing as sections were platted. Bob would have to request annexation at the appropriate time during their development so as to keep the City a viable unit. As is evident today and will be expanded on later, this trust was well placed and is one more of the significant factors allowing the growth of this Camelot.

In the November 20, 1986, regular FORHA meeting the 126 homeowners who were present unanimously adopted a resolution to proceed with a plan to incorporate Fair Oaks Ranch as required under law and to culminate the action as soon as possible. It was the desire of the homeowners that the development become one city eventually covering 5000 acres of the ranch.[5]

This resolution established the policy of the Association with regard to becoming a city. It read, in part,

"It is the long term interest of the homeowners in Fair Oaks Ranch to remain a single entity preferably incorporated at the appropriate time."

"It is not in our long term interest to be annexed either partially or in whole by either San Antonio or Boerne, but rather a 'Fair Oaks Township' or appropriate incorporated unit should be established to retain autonomy and the quality of life on the ranch." [6]

Elections were required to confirm the will of the homeowners affected and after countless hours of volunteer work these elections were held in January, 1987, in the north and April 1987 in the south. The time lapse was the result of administrative mechanics in the process of political activities of which we are all too familiar. Appropriate documents and applications had been assembled and submitted to the State of

Texas in the fall of 1986. What these documents requested was authority to create what became known as The City of Fair Oaks North and in April, 1987, to create what became known as The City of Fair Oaks South. With the favorable will of the homeowners in hand, the vision of a single autonomous governmental unit was put in motion. The plan was in the process of fulfillment. The City of Fair Oaks Ranch had reached the moment of birth.

But the elections to form two cities as a precursor to forming one city were very nearly trumped by an action of the San Antonio City Council in regular session before the voting had even begun. The FORHA officials had already applied to the state for approval to form the two cities before a December 18, 1986, San Antonio City Council meeting. Yet buried in the San Antonio City Council agenda for that day at item number 52 was an ordinance providing for the extension of the San Antonio city limits up the IH 10 corridor as had been discussed by the staff the previous spring. This extension of San Antonio city limits, if passed, would effectively prohibit the majority of the ranch from ever incorporating since that portion would be within San Antonio's extra-territorial jurisdiction.

According to David Deleranko, he had been reviewing the San Antonio City Council agendas on a regular basis anticipating the staff may try to move forward with their expansionist plans. His reviews proved prescient when he discovered item number 52 on that December 18 agenda. He contacted Robert Herring, now the newly elected FORHA President, and Don King, the soon to be Mayor of the North City of Fair Oaks Ranch and the planning director for the Association. They immediately registered to be heard at the San Antonio City Council meeting according to procedures in place. General Herring would be the spokesperson objecting to the extra-territorial expansion that would place the formation of the new city of Fair Oaks Ranch in jeopardy. His intent was to argue against the possible future annexation of the property of the development and officially advise the City of San Antonio of the petition to the U.S. Department of Justice to hold elections to create the two cities.

However, when the item came up for discussion Robert Herring was not provided any opportunity to talk to the City Council and the motion for extending the city limits of San Antonio was approved. This single vote made a portion of the Fair Oaks Ranch development officially a part of the City of San Antonio's extra-territorial jurisdiction and forfeited its autonomy.

By a stroke of luck, as some would conclude, before any additional actions could be taken by the City a staff employee approached the Mayor of San Antonio, Henry Cisneros who would later become the United States Secretary of Housing and Urban Development. The two had a brief, private and whispered discussion. At the completion of this discussion the Mayor instructed the Council that an administrative oversight had precluded a registered guest from speaking and invited Robert Herring to present his comments.

Following Robert Herring's comments, in which he outlined the steps the Fair Oaks Ranch Homeowners Association had already taken towards forming a city, the Council reconsidered their expansion plans and in essence de-annexed Fair Oaks

Ranch by agreeing to honor the results of the elections soon to be held. If the elections succeeded in supporting the formation of the two cities, they would honor the validity of the elections. If those elections failed to form the two cities as planned there would most likely be no cause for this book.

The elections mentioned earlier were then held and passed by the voters. With those elections completed and the two cities approved by the vote of the residents, the approval of county judges in the three counties in which the City's boundaries lay was required. The long and laborious journey to Camelot was not over but the completion was finally possible. The South city elected 'Boots' Gaubatz mayor of the larger of the two cities. Don King was elected mayor of the north. After all the suspense and activity and angst and work, the ranch was now officially two cities: Fair Oaks Ranch North and Fair Oaks Ranch South.

I have been unable to confirm this but the two cities may be the shortest lived incorporated cities in Texas history. As planned later that year the North voted on November 3, 1987, to request annexation by the City of Fair Oaks Ranch South. This was the first of many times that the principle called 'trust' was employed to the benefit of all.

The responsibility to fulfill their obligation then fell to the citizens of the City of Fair Oaks Ranch South who upheld the honor of trust and voted on January 3, 1988, to annex the City of Fair Oaks Ranch North thus achieving the goals set out nearly 2 years earlier - creating a single city known as Fair Oaks Ranch.

Chapter 5 — History Of Fair Oaks Ranch

Things on the Ranch were just getting started. The labor pains of birth would continue long after the City became an entity with a name and a penciled in spot on the map. But all the hard work was already paying dividends. The vision, the dream, the autonomy. They were all happening.

CHAPTER 6 – A LITTLE BIT OF HOME SCHOOLING

Forming a new city is a challenging activity but the founding fathers were about to discover that the real challenges had just begun. With the authority that comes with incorporation the onus of responsibility rolls through the front door like a hurricane on steroids. A significant number of issues were now on the table and each one of them demanded immediate attention. It was a daunting task.

Everyone who had volunteered to serve and was elected to the Council was new at this business. Every situation that arose required a quick study and many hours were spent in the books and in conversations with others who had travelled this road before. There were many meetings and numerous phone calls. Everyone involved in helping this city survive its birth worked overtime to help make it work. Every day brought a new situation to resolve. In reality the surprises would lessen although they would never end. But in the beginning, they occurred daily.

The City government was organized under the rules applicable to a general law city. The political apparatus consisted of a mayor and five aldermen. These six persons were responsible for creating a budget and setting a tax rate to support that budget. From the very beginning, these six people, or 'The Council' built a framework of financial conservatism that insisted on a balanced budget with provisions for a surplus against future needs. That approach is still in force today.

Complicating the management of the new City of Fair Oaks Ranch was the fact that it lay in three separate counties. This reality was unique and every step the new government took required the leaders to explore new territory. The City now owned the roads within its territory and the problems that came with ownership included maintaining them. Taxes, the bane of any form of government, had to be collected to support the services the City was created to provide. Fire protection, police protection, 'way of life' protection (believe it or not – a presumed right by some) were expected.

Each of the counties also had their own tax basis. Comal and Kendall County residents enjoyed a significantly lower tax rate than residents in Bexar County. This disparity was a bur under the saddle to many and remains so today. The City, including the portion south of Dietz Elkhorn Road, seems more aligned with Boerne and Kendall County than to Bexar County and the thought of sending tax dollars to a county for services never used or enjoyed was not a good feeling.

The unincorporated portions of the City had to be brought into the City in some fashion or the entire effort of forming the City was a waste. These large sections of property lay within the specially designed boundaries of the two cities that were now one. As already mentioned, they were protected from outside powers and had no reason to ask for the taxes that come with annexation. Trust continued as the primary and critical element of value in the entire enterprise.

Glenpool Inc. owned the water and its sister company, Elkhorn, owned the sewer company. These two entities controlled the rates and the response to a resident's request for service or repairs. As the ranch grew, the size of the system expanded to meet the requirements. The system of support provided by Ralph E. Fair, Inc., carried out by Bob Weiss, confirmed the quality commitment promised at the beginning. As a result, the new City was at least spared the complications of building and maintaining those two services. But that was to be for only a limited time as later events will reveal.

Another issue was San Antonio's finger annexation. As of this writing, the San Antonio City limit ends at two places of significance to Fair Oaks Ranch: one is just north of Leon Springs on IH 10 and the other is at the intersection of Ralph Fair Road and Dietz Elkhorn Road. Although the boundaries along IH 10 are marked by the ubiquitous green and white roadway signs, there are no signs that announce the boundaries on Ralph Fair Road. A strip of land five hundred feet wide on the east side of the road all the way to Leon Springs is within the City limits of San Antonio Texas. This little fact means that a five mile radius circle from both the IH 10 San Antonio city limit and the Ralph Fair-Dietz Elkhorn intersection in all directions belongs to San Antonio under the extra-territorial jurisdiction rules. This is even true as it pertained to Fair Oaks Ranch who normally would have had a half mile ETJ of its own.

To avoid a legal battle, the Founding Fathers signed a Memorandum of Agreement with San Antonio restricting growth outside the original 5,000 acres of the ranch. They agreed that the newly formed city would not seek to enforce its half mile jurisdiction outside the Fair Oaks Ranch city limits. The original plan promoted the position that the residents wanted to be who they were and nothing else. San Antonio once again agreed thus eliminating the imminent challenge of overseeing what would have been a half mile ETJ for Fair Oaks Ranch.[1] Things are always changing and future activity would ultimately prove the memorandum moot as I will relate in a later chapter.

First things first, however. The new city needed some place to conduct administrative duties and someone to do them. When the two small cities were formed, the City of Fair Oaks North operated out of a small, single room attached to the fire station at the entry to the Raintree Woods security section of the development. The City of Fair Oaks South operated out of a single, somewhat larger, room in the business office building at the corner of Fair Oaks Parkway and Dietz Elkhorn Road. When the two cities combined, the room in the business office building became the City Hall with two additional rooms upstairs: one for the Mayor to conduct appropriate business and the other for limited storage.[1]

The first city council was composed of the elected officials of the City of Fair Oaks Ranch South as that city had absorbed the City of Fair Oaks Ranch North. In effect, the City of Fair Oaks Ranch North and its council dissolved and the City of Fair Oaks Ranch South became the only authority for the community. Fair Oaks Ranch, with no north or south attached to it, was now the name of the entity. North and South were now only designations of where in the City a resident lived, generally. This would from time to time become an issue.

Council members were elected at large. The first council for the first city of Fair Oaks Ranch consisted of the Mayor, Boots Gaubatz, and five residents: James Buhaug, Bob Caldwell, Jim Deats, Wanda Price, and me - Gary Younglove. All these individuals were unpaid volunteers as was the City's first secretary, Donna Younglove, who voluntarily filled in for three months until the Council was able to recruit a paid employee.[2]

In the true fashion of an involved manager and as evidence of Boots Gaubatz's organizational skills he led the Council in forming numerous volunteer committees each under the leadership of an appointed chairman and overseen by a Council member. A planning committee and a postal service committee were among the first actions taken during the first few months of the City's existence. Also the Council appointed a tax coordinator, an emergency services director and a volunteer coordinator. Each member of the Council was also active as a project manager for a number of projects, each pursuing solutions to various facets of setting up a strong, functioning city. Some of the early successes included a franchise agreement with Southwestern Bell that provided much needed income and an EMS contract with an ambulance company providing a much needed service.[3]

Because there was no paid staff at the time, selected council members were appointed to manage certain functions required but with no committee required to carry them out. These functions included the normal duties such as Treasurer, Secretary, Insurance, Administration, and such. Every Alderman also was required to serve on the 'Figure Out How To Do It Cheaper And Better Without Increasing Taxes Committee'.

The priority in the first few months, however, was police service arrangements. Without its own police force the City was under the jurisdiction of Bexar, Kendall, and Comal counties depending on where you lived. Responses to calls for assistance from residents were handled by the sheriffs in each of these three counties. In Bexar County it often took over an hour for a Sheriff's Deputy to respond to a burglar alarm as it did to me on one false alarm occasion. It was not the fault of the Sheriff's office. The Deputies had an enormous territory to cover and Fair Oaks Ranch was in the northwest extremity of the county. If the Deputy was on call elsewhere, say in the southern portion of the county, he would have to travel over 40 miles to answer the call. And when it is a false alarm, you can understand the deputy's frustration.

This situation was, of course, not acceptable to the newly formed City Council and its Mayor nor was the Bexar Country Sheriff, for example, anxious to race into the hills in pursuit of a false alarm. So the Council immediately began the process of finding a better solution within the very limited budget they had. And by May 1, 1988, just over three months after incorporation, they had a solution, even if purposely temporary, in place.

It was not an ideal solution but it was a giant step in the right direction. It would be improved over time with a series of interim solutions until the police force in place now was established. But Fair Oaks Ranch had a law enforcement officer dedicated to the City. By signing a contract with Jerry Connell, Precinct #2, Bexar County, an officer with the full authority of the City would be on patrol 24 hours a day throughout the City including the Security area - Raintree Woods. The fully commissioned police officers on duty were under the supervision of Constable Jerry Connell who was overseen by the Volunteer Director of Emergency Services, Ron Rogers, a retired law enforcement officer and resident of the City. The Constables had the authority to handle all matters just as though they were part of an established police force.[4] The first priority of the new city was completed – at least for a period of time that allowed the Council to focus on other urgent needs.

Chapter 6 — History Of Fair Oaks Ranch

There was not that much crime in the area but having a response just minutes away was a duty and responsibility of a functioning city. In fact, in 1988 throughout all of the 5,000 acres of the ranch, the crime rate was one of the lowest in Texas and possibly the nation. The distance from San Antonio and heavy population centers may have been a contributing factor. Don't let the naysayers hear of that. They were still trying to figure out how we became so good at being too far away.

The City Council wanted to ensure that the crime rate remained low and the presence of an officer of the law 24 hours a day was a good way to do so. The diversity of coverage in the past was now a thing of the past. It was now possible to call one number for assistance and have nearly immediate response. It's a comfort knowing you have someone of authority nearby and to this day the need for serious, immediate response is rare. That's what life in Camelot is all about.

CHAPTER 7 - THE CENSUS DON'T KNOW

In 1980 the population of the development was a mere 541.[1] But this small number belies the success of the development since its beginning only six years earlier. In that short period of time, a ranch once thought to be too remote from San Antonio to have any chance of success as a development, was proving all the pundits wrong.

The sales of the properties north of the Cibolo Creek had been so successful that numerous persons, as mentioned earlier, competed for the same piece of land. As a result, the names of potential buyers were placed on lists from which the lucky few would be chosen in drawings for the separate parcels of land.[2] It was only the beginning and by 1985, growth along the IH

10 corridor was rapid and becoming a concern to many in the area. As a result, a Kendall County task force was established and headed by County Judge Ken Muller. The purpose of this Economic Growth Task Force was to "promote economic development along Interstate 10" from Seguin on the east side of San Antonio to as far west as Kerrville.

Not everyone was in agreement with the assessment that growth was on its way. In fact, the head of the task force, Judge Muller, told the task force members at their first meeting that he felt most people in Kendall County did not want development along IH-10 and that only the property owners who stood to gain from rising real estate prices would be in favor. He believed billboards were the prime industry along the corridor and there wasn't much going on then or would be going on for years. [3]

Most members of the task force disagreed with the Judge and ultimately were proven right in their opposing position. The 541 population in Fair Oaks Ranch was only the beginning of what was to become an era of rapid and substantial growth that would forever change the looks and the character of the 16 mile stretch of IH-10 and its surrounding land from FM 1604 (later renamed Loop 1604) to just north of Boerne.[3]

By 1987 when the cities of Fair Oaks Ranch North and Fair Oaks Ranch South were formed and voted into existence, the population on the ranch had grown to an estimated 1,800 souls. This equates to an annual growth rate of more than 20% annually. The growth continued on this explosive path until in 2012 an estimate 6,000 plus residents lived here.

With a growing population and a requirement to provide essential services to the residents, the two sister cities began the onerous task of collecting taxes and establishing governments for the short term that would extend into the future when the long range plans for consolidation came to fruition. In that regard a tax rate of 25 cents per $100 of real estate value was enacted in both of the short lived fledgling cities. Because of the tri-county location of the two cities, appraisals were carried out by different entities – Kendall and Comal Appraisal Districts in the north and Bexar Appraisal District in the south. Fortunately, the two city governments had acted early on to preclude the confusion of separate billing entities. Although the assessments would be performed separately the tax collector would be a single authority due to the preparation of a contract with Kendall Appraisal District to bill and collect all City taxes due regardless of the county of residence.

The tax rate of 25 cents per hundred dollars of value was one of the lowest tax rates in the State at the time and remains low to this day. It was the stated policy of both city councils that taxes should be levied only for essential services and should be kept at the lowest possible rate. The ability to keep the rate at a minimum was heavily dependent on the contributions of the many volunteers involved in the City's operation. Their service, without compensation, became a major factor in keeping taxes low. And the sense of community involvement and commitment to making the City prosper was evident throughout the beginning years of incorporation.

The City of Fair Oaks North had as its primary mission a single goal: to petition the City of Fair Oaks South for

Chapter 7   History Of Fair Oaks Ranch

annexation thus leading to the dissolution of itself. As has been already discussed, work on that mission began immediately after the City's formation and an election in November 1987 affirmed the residents' approval of the action.

Although Boots Gaubatz, Don King, and Robert Herring are considered the Founding Fathers, the Councils of both the north and the south were instrumental in keeping the effort on track during its most vulnerable period. The Aldermen of the two cities were as follows:

City of Fair Oaks Ranch North	**City of Fair Oaks Ranch South**
Don King – Mayor	Boots Gaubatz - Mayor
Ray Arnold	Jim Buhaug
Chet Campbell	Bob Caldwell
Frank Hannibal	Jim Deats
Sam Sedki	Wanda Price
Linda Tom	Gary Younglove
Richard Slocomb – Marshall	Don Zook - Marshall

While Fair Oaks Ranch North was working to achieve its own annexation, Fair Oaks Ranch South proceeded to establish a fully functioning government. With no data on costs associated with managing a new city, the Council developed a budget of $177,000 and set a tax rate to fit within that budget – something unusual in government these days. Since the security of the citizens was a priority for the Mayor and Council, work began immediately to study options available. Both the north and the south worked together on the issue. Chet Campbell from the North's council and Don Zook, Town

Marshall for the South, completed extensive research concerning costs, coverage, and other details of this important service. They had a January 1, 1988, target.[4]

During this period, Mayor Boots Gaubatz began what was to become a regular and beneficial practice and an example of his commitment to open government operations. He published his first Report To The Citizens newsletter informing the residents of what their new city government was doing. In this initial communication, the tone of the governing body was clearly stated:

Many days and hours have been spent bringing us to this point where we can see our goal - one City for all Fair Oaks, with home rule, quality of life and taxes only a fraction of either San Antonio or Boerne...we are dedicated to high services and low taxes...we will do our best to keep you informed...you are welcome at meetings and calls to me or Council Members are encouraged...

As added evidence that this government was going to be open and responsive to the needs and desires of the citizens, Mayor Gaubatz provided not only the only City Office phone number to all residents but also his work, home, and mobile phone numbers. Back then a mobile phone was a treasured communication device not widely available as it is today. Freely publishing the number was something unheard of. These numbers remained available throughout his long tenure as Mayor and he never failed to accept or respond to the many calls he received.

The Mayor and the Aldermen were committed to making this

experiment, as some would call it, work. Most of the Council held full time jobs and worked on Council activities in the evenings and on weekends. It is testament to their conviction that it was worth the many hours on end working out the details of how to make a ship as large as what they had boarded slide smoothly through the rough seas of creation.

The astounding success of the volunteer program came as a surprise to many. There was a ready supply of residents who wanted to help make this effort succeed. Later on I list the many committees, activities, and positions for which the young city didn't have funds to support paid employees to carry out. Each of those responsibilities was handled by a volunteer. This was truly a community of cooperation.

The last issue of the newsletter for the year of 1987 was a discussion on the name for the City that would be formed by virtue of the consolidation. There were two options on the table: Fair Oaks or Fair Oaks Ranch. Recommendations were solicited and discussions continued into 1988. Those discussions and the results of a straw vote are covered in the next chapter along with the birth of the single city and its infant years.

There has not been enough recognition of the invaluable support the volunteers provided over the years. Everyone involved in the beginning and throughout the formative period sacrificed to make this city survive. Under the Volunteer section at the back of this book is a list of all those I could garner from research and available documents. I know I have missed some and to those I haven't listed, I apologize. Your efforts are still very much appreciated.

The City was taking shape and the early months were navigated with expert planning and conscious commitment to success. Despite the odds against the City making a good go of it, all those involved in its birth deserve credit for persevering against those odds. The City was – is – and will remain a positive force in the expanded community for a long, long time due to the efforts of many during its formative era.

Chapter 7

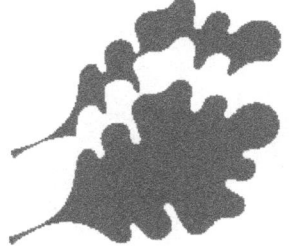

CHAPTER 8 – ONE PLUS ONE = ONE

With the November 1987 elections in the north completed, the request for annexation by the south delivered, elections by the residents in the south to accept the request for annexation finished, the efforts of hundreds of people over more than two years was finally realized. On January 21, 1988, the formation of a single city was complete. However, the task of managing a growing city with all the appurtenant problems and rewards was just beginning. With the annexation of the north, the south council assumed leadership of the single city and the North's Council was disbanded. The South Council's life was to be rather short, however, as new elections were required to select a single city council elected by both north and south residents.

These elections would take place during the normal election cycle in May 1988.

In the meantime, actions begun by the south in preparation for the consolidation continued. First and foremost on everyone's mind was the need for adequate police protection and services. The effort, briefly discussed in an earlier chapter, had been started the previous year with a combined north/south study of options. The recommendations of the task force appointed for this purpose were among the first items on the new council's agenda.

Initially, the City began negotiations with Bexar County to provide law enforcement services through the Bexar County Sheriff's office. It was a logical option as the majority of the residents lived in Bexar County. These negotiations addressed a contractual arrangement wherein the sheriff would staff one patrol unit in the City, 365 days a year, on a 24 hour day basis.[1] The services would include:

- Responding to calls for law enforcement services by citizens.

- Preventive patrol activities.

- Traffic law enforcement.

- Community crime prevention services.

- Conducting investigations of reported felonies which occur in the City.

All the officers assigned to the City were to be full-time personnel who were licensed peace officers and under the supervision of the Sheriff's office. Although under the control of the Sheriff for police activities, they would remain assigned to the City of Fair Oaks Ranch.

The City was unable to complete these negotiations. There were too many bureaucratic obstacles in the way to allow the process to work smoothly and, as discussed earlier, the City turned instead to Jerry Connell, the Bexar County Constable for Precinct #2.

When the negotiations with the Constable proved successful, all of the services listed above were included in a contract signed by the City and the Constable. Police services began on May 1, 1988. The planning model had estimated the cost for this contract would be approximately $140,000 yearly. However, when all the dust settled, the actual cost was only $117,000 and the City's top priority was now complete. Boots told the residents: "We have studied many options over the last months and this is the best service at the lowest cost with coverage our residents asked for".[2]

Strange as it may seem, a debate over what to name the City was next. The debate had begun almost as soon as the ink documenting the City's formation had dried. There were two views with both sides expressing strong feelings for their choice. Some residents preferred the name to be simply Fair Oaks while others preferred it to remain Fair Oaks Ranch. The argument for the change to the two word name included a feeling the name was too long as well as the fact that most people referred to the City as simply Fair Oaks anyway. Opponents of the change argued that there was already a Texas Community named Fair Oaks (about 60 miles east of Waco near the intersection of SH 164 and FM 39). Because that community was unincorporated, Fair Oaks Ranch could pre-empt that smaller community and take the name but it was not in keeping with the character of Fair Oaks Ranch. Further, they argued that the nationally known Fair Oaks, California, already had strong name recognition.[3]

The Council could have simply made a decision but the Mayor put it to the test and scheduled a straw vote to coincide with the general elections on May 7, 1988. The results of the non-binding vote were 281 votes for keeping Ranch in the name and 76 votes for removing Ranch from the name. No further discussions ensued and the name remained unchanged. It seems strange that, although this debate resulted in keeping Ranch as part of the name, vendors and others throughout the country will invariably drop the 'Ranch' from their address labels and other identification documents when dealing with the City.

By the end of the first year of this fledgling city the Council and Mayor had completed the creation and organization of more than 20 committees focusing on specific aspects of the City's operation. As a testimony to the spirit of volunteerism within the City each of these committees, under the oversight of a council member was headed by a volunteer and was composed entirely of volunteers. The specific committees and volunteer positions were as follows:

- Fair Oaks Ranch Celebration
- City Planning, Land Use, Codes, Etc.
- Emergency Services
- Judge for May 7 (1988) Election
- Telephone Calling Scope
- Fair Oaks Ranch Mail Service
- Fire Protection
- EMS and 911
- Insurance Services
- Tax Administration
- Franchise Tax
- Street Commissioner
- City Historian
- Animal Control
- Public and Community Relations
- Volunteer Services
- Administration and Treasurer
- City Secretary[4]

As can be seen, each of these committee volunteer positions focused on a particular segment of the City's operation. There is a significant number of activities that come with incorporation and the demands of the residents do not abate once a government has been formed to deal with the issues a single resident has little power to handle. Within months of the City's formation, however, significant progress had been made in setting up a smooth and efficient city Government with all these new functions at least making progress toward smooth implementation.

Before the first year was over the City would have an EMS

contract for services within the City, police service provided by contract, a franchise agreement with Southwestern Bell that would provide additional income, a full-time city secretary, the beginnings of a library of ordinances providing for the services residents desired, an agreement with the Texas Department of Transportation (TXDOT) to perform a traffic study, a local polling place for the Boerne Independent School District elections, a municipal court, and a multitude of other minor activities that filled in gaps in this newly formed community.

A significant accomplishment that would carry through the first 25 years of the City's existence was the completion of a budget that mirrored the philosophy of the City's financial approach from the very beginning. The Mayor and the Council were committed to operating the City with a surplus and using that surplus to build a reserve over time that would allow the City to operate up to six months without any revenue. This was accomplished in this first year with a tax rate of .25 per $100 property valuation. Following that first year's success the new $415,750 budget for the second year of the City's operation included a reduced tax rate of .23 per $100 valuation while still providing the surplus necessary to build a reserve.

During the same period the City purchased its first police car to be used by the Constable officer under contract. Within the first six months the costs of car allowances under the contract had exceeded expectations and this purchase allowed the City to achieve considerable savings in reimbursable expenses in spite of the cost of the vehicle. It would be the first of many actions taken over the next few years leading up to the establishment of the City's own police force.

This and many more firsts would become the norm for this new city as it worked to get on its feet and setup house in the foothills of the Hill Country. But the first year as a city was now a thing of the past. The organization of the City was beginning to hit its stride. Procedures and processes were shaping up and the City entered an era akin to adolescence. Typical of that period in a youngster's life there would be many issues to deal with. And that is the subject of Part Three of this book.

Chapter 8   History Of Fair Oaks Ranch

PART THREE

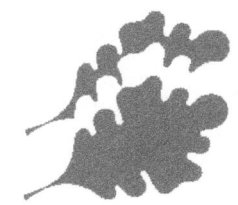

THE FOLLOW-THROUGH

If a newly formed city is to succeed it must follow through with its published purpose and put down roots for the future. In this respect Fair Oaks Ranch was no different than any other city formed in the past. However, it did have one thing going for it that many of the other cities didn't. Fair Oaks Ranch was built on the premise that the government was established to protect the citizens, provide only the services the citizens wanted, to do so at the lowest possible cost, and to stay out of the citizens way except for issues of health and safety.

Complying with this mission as a new city was not an easy task but it was the passion of all the volunteers and the City Council. This section discusses just a few of the myriad things that took place during this period of adolescence. Each of the items discussed here is only the tip of the iceberg but demonstrates the commitment to financial conservatism and unobtrusive government held by all involved.

Part Three   History Of Fair Oaks Ranch

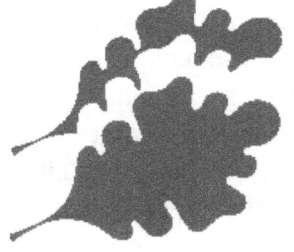

CHAPTER 9 – SETTING UP HOUSE

Now that the two cities were combined into a single entity and the first year of operation had settled into a functional process, work began in earnest to establish the dream of its forefathers in a solid foundation of reality.

The Mayor assumed the functions of both the political leader for the fledgling operation and the City Supervisor overseeing the day to day operation of all that was soon to happen. Mayor 'Boots' Gaubatz promised the residents a government with as little intrusion in the resident's daily lives as possible. He was committed to providing governmental services that would leave the resident free from the constraints normally ushered in by a local government out of control. The forefathers' dream of self-governance was now a reality and they wanted to build on that dream without outside intervention or inside coercion.

To help with the efforts to keep taxes low as well as to avoid unnecessary expenses, the members of the first city council dedicated their efforts in two important ways. Firstly, they served without compensation of any kind, as also did the Mayor. This is a tradition that continues to the current day. Secondly, each of the Aldermen assumed responsibility for managing some aspect of the City's operation - again with no compensation of any kind. These functions, as listed in the previous chapter were not minimal. Duties such as street maintenance consumed large amounts of time as the City had just inherited over 30 miles of roadway and needed to ensure a high level of quality from the start.

Other significant efforts involved animal control, providing for fire protection services, ensuring the continuation of quality water, then provided by the privately held Glenpool, Inc. water company that Ralph Fair, Jr., and Don Smith had the foresight to establish. Other activities such as tax administration, developing an accounting system within a limited budget, arranging for emergency services and the like provided the Council and the many volunteers who wanted to help many challenges during the first year and a half of the City's adolescence. It was a busy and an exciting time with some new requirement or surprise popping up nearly every day.

Among the very first requirements was to hire the City's first paid employee. There was a plethora of administrative requirements and duties that the City needed to complete to meet State mandates that come with local governing authority. That first employee was the City Secretary. Linda Zartler, an efficient and dedicated employee, filled that position and helped guide the City through many sticky wickets of city founding.

"We were developing (the City) as things popped up," she commented during a recent conversation. "We didn't have any ordinances. We were like an adolescent learning the rules. Nothing was in place. Everything was *learn as you go*."

What is perhaps the most telling of the earlier events was her help in setting up an accounting system. One of my Council duties was overseeing the financial aspects of the City. To manage the budgeting processes at minimal cost, we purchased a $39.00 piece of software known to this day as Quicken and designed for use primarily in the home. Together, Linda Zartler and I worked on adapting the system for city use and after only a few weeks were able to bend it to our will. This software turned out to be exceptionally useful in its modified role and was used by the City until the late 1990s. To this day I don't think Intuit, the Quicken organization, intended it to be used as we did. They would have preferred we use the more expensive Quickbooks program.

"We were doing everything," Zartler recalls. "Of course, life was a lot simpler then at the very beginning. We didn't have animal control, police, maintenance, building codes, and all those things that help you tear your hair out." As an example some of the residents in the early days had a unique view of the purpose of their new city government. "Because we were in basically a fairly affluent neighborhood," Linda said. "There were some people who felt I was there to sweep the street in front of their house or clean up around their house after a heavy rain." Her experiences and abilities helped her eventually land a job with the City of Boerne, Texas, in 1995 where she is currently employed as the Administration Services Director.

The early years also saw the beginning of a tradition which would be carried on throughout the City's 25 years existence – birthday parties. These anniversary celebrations began less than three months after the formation of the City of Fair Oaks Ranch with the first one being held on April 9, 1988. City officials and local dignitaries were introduced to the attendees who then partook of a barbecue dinner served up as usual by volunteers from within the City. Mayor Gaubatz's comments at this first celebration included a phrase that he would use frequently throughout his tenure. It set the tone for Fair Oaks Ranch governance: "…the best government is the least government…"

In true style for a city that has a lot to be proud of, the celebration drew a crowd of over 500 and a small parade was organized along with a display of antique and rare cars. Held on the grounds of the Homeowners Park at the intersection of Pimlico and Rocking Horse (later named for Norman Vestal, a volunteer who  devoted significant amounts of time maintaining the park and other City properties), it was like a scene out of the movie State Fair. The tradition continued yearly until switching to a five year interval in 1998.

Rounding out the early years of the combined city's existence a series of other firsts made it into the history-filled newsletters. The City received approval to establish a polling place for elections within the corporate city limits, completed a survey of street signs, established a long range plan for road maintenance, completed an expansion of the fire station on Fair Oaks Parkway, and completed striping on the parkway thus reducing confusion as to the number of lanes available for vehicles.

Moving into 1989, a significant achievement was a contract with the Leon Springs Volunteer Fire Department, the fire protection service covering the City's area. For years the Volunteer Fire Department depended on donations from the community to support its operations. These donations were often insufficient to maintain the quality of service desired. Additionally, not everyone donated. As a result, many residents were subsidizing other residents. The Mayor and Council decided to address these concerns early on. They negotiated a contract with the fire department that supplanted the annual fund drive and resulted in everyone in the City sharing the cost of maintaining fire protection services equally. All this was done without any increase in taxes – keeping faith with the original budgetary commitment.

Along with the fire department contract, work progressed on getting E911 services implemented for the entire city. After weeks of discussions and council involvement, the service was made available to all residents on March 27, 1989. The little community that was too far from San Antonio to be viable was moving into the 20th century with a speed that often defied understanding.

In May 1989, the City held its first full term election since its formation and set up the structure to ensure staggered terms for the Mayor and council persons. Not only was it the first full term election, but it was also the first of many elections wherein the incumbents were unopposed – an occurrence that would be repeated for almost every election in the City's history. This in itself was evidence that the leadership for the City was on the right track. The continuity that resulted was especially valuable to keeping the promises made to the residents – low overhead and costs combined with limited government.

During this time, the Council approved a mission statement for the City that I drafted as part of my Director of Administration and Planning duties. We held annual planning sessions and the mission statement was an offshoot of the deliberations during the very first session held in the fall of 1988. This mission which holds to this day was refined and endorsed by the Council and published as a constitution-like document to guide the leadership into the future. Included here, it is important in its simplicity and stated purpose of hands off, non-intrusive government:

MISSION OF THE CITY OF FAIR OAKS RANCH

To provide and enhance those quality of life factors which influenced the citizens to establish a residence within the City and to provide security, public safety, and police services for the maintenance of good order and the protection of personal and real property located within the City limits.

PRIORITIES

- Take no action that would materially affect the quality of life in any fashion detrimental to the continuance and enhancement of conditions existing at the time the City was incorporated.

- Pursue a long range plan that will protect the autonomy of the City, provide for the inclusion of unincorporated areas in the City, and promote the City's authority to determine its own future.

- Contract with a law enforcement agency at a reasonable cost for the security of the citizens and the protection of personal and real property within the City limits.

- Provide for reliable emergency services through arrangement with existing Emergency Medical Services agencies.

- Provide for reliable fire protection services through arrangement with existing fire protection agencies.

- Build appropriate reserve funds necessary to meet large expenditure requirements, such as road repair, with regular deposits so as to have as little effect on tax rates and the least reliance on debt creation as possible.

- Conduct services consistent with the above listed priorities in the most cost effective manner possible, to include extensive use of volunteers, so as to keep the tax rate as low as possible.[2]

Twenty-five years later that original mission is still in effect with only one minor change to the priority concerning contract for law enforcement. With its own police department in place, that priority was changed from a contracting emphasis to a maintenance emphasis. And as evidenced by the low tax rate, surplus funds in reserve, and police and fire and medical emergency services in place, it has obviously been followed closely by all the Councils since its adoption.

Prior to mid-1989 the residents of the City had to use Boerne as their city of residence because the post office that served the City was in Boerne. Many residents thought that, as an incorporated city, we should have our own post office. The Council agreed and began the effort of obtaining the City's own post office. Unfortunately, the financial circumstances that faced the United States Postal Service were not conducive to establishing any office outside Boerne and the effort failed.

Undeterred, the City pursued the next best thing and in the summer of 1989 the USPS granted all Fair Oaks Ranch residences the approval to use Fair Oaks Ranch instead of Boerne in their address. As many of us are reminded from time to time and, as mentioned earlier, many commercial entities continue to drop the Ranch from the name and many even still use Boerne in spite of our efforts to educate them. Apparently, it's the lazy way out as both Boerne and Fair Oaks Ranch show up in the mailing programs and Boerne comes first.

Another interesting first was the contract reached with the Boerne library that allowed Fair Oaks Ranch residents to use the library without having to pay membership fees. Although not in existence at the time of this writing, this contract provided the library an allocation of funds based on the average past usage by Fair Oaks Ranch residents. It allowed any resident free access to the library facilities and was an ancillary benefit to many of the residents who were regular visitors to the library.

The City continued to become involved in more and more of the activities of the local area. Of note was the obtaining of a seat on the Kendall County Appraisal District Board of Directors. As will be covered later, this position was beneficial to the City when resolving confusing and non-complementary property valuation assessments that were completed with the City included in three different assessor authorities.

In late 1989 it became apparent that hiring outside contractors to complete the many maintenance projects in the City was not the most cost effective way to go. As a result, Donald Belzung was hired as the first outside maintenance employee for the City. As such, his one-man job kept him immersed in any number of duties. It became apparent in short order that one person could not keep up with the growing demands for services in the growing city and additional employees were hired to assist him. Today, with the significantly expanded maintenance activities required by a city whose population is more than four times what it was back then, that maintenance force has grown to six employees in a variety of disciplines.

The era of firsts for the new city was just gathering steam as 1989 drew to a close. Many more firsts were in store over the next three years and only then would it become an era of seconds and more. Before then, however, work continued on building a strong yet unobtrusive local government that all the residents expected when they voted to avoid annexation by San Antonio.

Like all new communities there were growing pains but none like older and larger communities face seemingly on a daily basis. It was in the fall of 1989, almost two years after the City's founding, that the City suffered its first vandalism event and that was minor. A number of street signs were stolen and some damaged. Certainly the acts of younger residents or visitors. And then a period of non-vandalism ensued that would last for years.

That fall Fair Oaks Ranch entered into another contract with an organization that had been serving the community since its beginning – The Hill Country Animal League. This organization managed by Lynn Buhaug, the wife of one of the City's original councilmen, provided animal control and rescue services to the City on a volunteer basis before the contract and, like the fire department, depended on contributions for existence. With the contract, the League became our primary animal issues 'go to' organization for many years.

Early in 1990, the Council established a Beautification Committee and appointed Alderwoman Wanda Price as its chairwoman. The first ever city landscaping activity then took place and that activity is still in evidence on Fair Oaks Parkway. Wanda organized a group of concerned citizens and they planted an Afghan Pine on the parkway's median near  the intersection of Dietz Elkhorn and Fair Oaks Parkway. That tree has survived the floods and droughts we have suffered over the years and is today a good specimen for all who drive by the office building at that intersection. It is the second and western-most of the two pines near that intersection.

As time passed and the City operations began to take on the smoothness of a well-organized function, it became apparent that a central waste collection business was in order. The Fair Oaks Ranch Homeowners Association was managing this function and had approached the City with the idea of beginning a recycling effort combined with normal garbage collection. As a result of discussions in this regard, the City assumed responsibility for the function. In short order, Garbage Gobbler and the City reached an agreement that would apply to the entire city for a fixed monthly fee. The agreement included weekly pickup of both non-recyclable and

Chapter 9   History Of Fair Oaks Ranch

recyclable trash and a semi-annual large item and brush pick up at no extra cost to the residents. Similar contracts have been in effect throughout the City's life with all three companies who have performed these services.

The pace of activity and the number of new issues facing the City and the Council was staggering. Yet, the hands off approach to governing unless involvement was absolutely necessary or in the best interests of the residents was working well.

Street lights were installed at CPSEnergy expense (known simply as CPS or City Public Service back then) at the entrances to Fair Oaks Ranch from Ralph Fair Road, entrances that were especially dark and had the propensity for accidents late at night. The first reported case of Oak Wilt in the City was proven inaccurate. The first city float to take part in the Kendall County Fair Parade rolled down Main Street in Boerne. The area code in the Bexar County properties changed from 512 to 210. The first voting precinct for Bexar County residents in the City was established. And the first severe rainfall of 7 inches in 1.5 hours and resulting flood cut the City in two at the Cibolo Creek crossing on Ralph Fair Road.

These items were among many others[1] that attracted only minimal historical attention due to their routine nature. But among them were some very significant actions that these others mingled with. The issues of appropriate city facilities, deer management, annexation of the Pfieffer area along the Parkway, Texas Department of Transportation response to Cibolo Creek flooding, planning for establishment of an internal police department, and a significant disagreement with the Boerne ISD Board of Directors dominated the government landscape in the final years of this early era of firsts. Some of the more interesting activities will form the basis of the next few chapters.

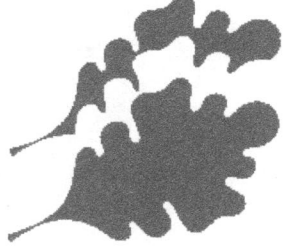

CHAPTER 10 – DON'T MESS WITH *FAIR OAKS RANCH* TEXAS

The State of Texas educational system is organized around a number of independent school districts. The State Board of Education (SBOE), an elected 15 member board, and the Commissioner of Education oversee the public education system of Texas in accordance with the Texas Education Code. This board oversees more than 250 school districts throughout Texas.[1]

Each of these several independent school districts is governed locally by a board composed of three to seven elected persons called trustees who are resident within the district. As a general rule this board of trustees has the exclusive power and duty to govern and oversee the management of the public schools of the district.[2]

Among many other duties incumbent on the trustees are several that were of significant debate in the early years of the City. Three of those duties that had an interesting and agitating impact on Fair Oaks Ranch residents are stated here and include the Board's responsibility to:

> - seek to establish working relationships with other public entities to make effective use of community resources and to serve the needs of public school students in the community.
>
> - adopt a process through which district personnel, students or the parents or guardians of students and members of the public may obtain a hearing from the district administrators and the board regarding a complaint.
>
> - not act individually on behalf of the board unless authorized by the board.[2]

The Boerne Independent School District (BISD) was once known as the Boerne County Line ISD since its geographical boundaries crossed the county lines of Bexar and Kendall much as the City does today. The name was changed to the simpler moniker of Boerne ISD in the late 80s without any change in the boundaries. These boundaries do not follow any naturally defined direction except for two portions that follow the county lines between Kendall County and both Bandera and Comal Counties. In short, it includes the southern half of Kendall County with a section reaching to the north toward

History Of Fair Oaks Ranch   Chapter 10

the northeast border with Blanco County and a portion of northwest Bexar County.[3]

Events within Fair Oaks Ranch were still on a fast track in the fall of 1991 with many goals achieved and many more still in the process of completion. The promised limited government was, in fact, a reality and the balanced budget approach to income and expense was applied without exception. The Council believed in a pay-as-you-go method of operation and in making the process of governing as easy as possible. Part of that approach resulted in the establishment of polling places for general and school district elections in the City so residents would not have to travel to vote for city officials in one location, other local officials in another location, and school board trustees in a third location – all on the same day. Had that travel been necessary it would certainly have reduced voter participation.

It worked well for all involved and provided an efficient and convenient process of voting in the City. That well supported process was soon to be placed in jeopardy during the City's period of adolescence. At that time the Boerne ISD Board of Trustees, following a recent election, was chaired by Corky Corcoran with Rosemary Piper, Ray Lee, Erwin "Diz" Reeves, Jim Deats (a one time Fair Oaks Ranch Alderman), Millie Bergman, and Pam Plunkett serving as trustees.

There had been a recent challenge to the board's authority to dictate school dress requirements by some of the high school students and their parents. And the dialogue between the Board of Trustees and the parents and students became a matter of intense public interest. Fair Oaks Ranch soon found itself in the middle of this fray although it had nothing to do with the City.

At issue was a ruling the Board had made concerning hair styles a few of the boys at Boerne High School were sporting. In the conservative community that Boerne was at the time, earrings on male secondary students were prohibited and the only acceptable hair length for boys was that which did not reach below the collar of a dress shirt. In a display of youthful rebellion, a few of the students disregarded the rule and defied the Board. It is interesting to note that all of the boys involved in this little rebellion 'back then' are quite successful men in business today.

The rebellion of these students led to an eventual confrontation between the Board and those it was sworn to support that consumed Boerne and the surrounding area for many weeks. In fact, the incident received national news coverage and a trip to New York City for the BISD Superintendent Joe Doentges with a number of the boys for a taped interview for the then Maury Povich show.[4]

The boys involved in the protest were not of the character many people usually associate with protesters. They were honor roll students, respectful of authority, willing to follow the rules, and all destined to graduate from college and go on to successful careers. They believed in the concept of free choice and merely wanted to voice their objections to what they thought was an onerous rule.[5] Their actions would draw the new 'City to the South – Fair Oaks Ranch' into its first and only serious conflict with the 'City to the North - Boerne'. It turned into what we can now look back and see as something humorous although it was far from that 'back then'.

With all the foregoing as prelude, the real stuff begins. The City discovered, without any advance warning, that Trustee Rosemary Piper had added an item to the September 16, 1991, meeting agenda that would eliminate the Boerne ISD polling place in Fair Oaks Ranch that the Council had worked so hard to put in place. The board was already in a stage of heightened stress with the young men protesting the hair length rule and many Fair Oaks Ranch residents believed that the Board's action was politically motivated.

This accusation was somewhat substantiated when Board member Piper and Kendall County Taxpayer's League representative Arthur Mace wrote a letter suggesting the children of Fair Oaks Ranch residents had been used to convey unfair campaign data to their parents therefore helping Fair Oaks Ranch voters affect the election outcome against the League's candidates.

Mayor 'Boots' Gaubatz immediately prepared a defense of the previously approved voting precinct and appeared before the Board on the City's behalf. It was coincidental that the student dress code issue was up for debate at the same meeting with some of the students exercising their right to address the Board. In that regard, the meeting place was quickly filled with dress code protesters as well as Fair Oaks Ranch residents protesting the removal of the voting polling place in the City.

With standing room only and open windows along the side of the room for scores of others outside to hear the proceedings, both the students and the Mayor gave their comments amid the often vocal comments of support and exuberant applause erupting in the tense atmosphere of the cramped room.

The Board seemed frustrated by the show of support for the protesters. The efforts of the Board Chairman to restrict those who wanted to comment or question proposed actions brought instant disapproval from those in attendance. It seemed predestined that the atmosphere would take on a more sinister mood and many of those in attendance eventually became frustrated as well and boycotted the meeting by walking out.

In the end, both the students and the Mayor of Fair Oaks Ranch lost their arguments to the board who voted to uphold both the dress code and the motion to remove the Fair Oaks Ranch polling location and consolidate it with one in the Boerne locale. The dress code issue soon melted into history but the polling place had new legs and would be in the news for some weeks to come.

The Fair Oaks Ranch City Council immediately approved a proposal to have the City Attorney send letters to the Justice Department and to Boerne ISD president 'Corky' Corcoran protesting the board's 4-3 decision. The school board also wrote the Justice Department at the same time asking for the required approval to implement its decision.[6]

Time to back off and wait, right? Not so. While awaiting the Justice Department's response to the letters submitted, Board member Ray Lee, who had voted in favor of the consolidation, requested that the subject be included in the upcoming

October board meeting agenda. Why he did so remains unknown but Mayor Gaubatz comments to the Board that his contacts in various government and attorney circles informed him the odds are heavily in favor of a rejection by the Justice Department certainly had to have had an influence.

Once the September meeting had adjourned and the Council had directed the attorney to protest the action, the City began collecting signatures on a petition also protesting the action. The Mayor took that petition to the October board meeting and presented the petition with 912 names requesting the restoration of the Fair Oaks Ranch polling place.

With one trustee absent, the Board then voted unanimously to restore the polling place.[7] And like the dress code issue, the polling place issue faded into news history. Unfortunately, the bad taste left in many participants' mouths took much longer to dissipate. It is a true symbol of this community's desire to remain a Camelot and the supportive leadership in both Boerne and the school district that any hard feelings are no longer evident in the superb relation we have with our neighbors to the north.

Chapter 10 History Of Fair Oaks Ranch

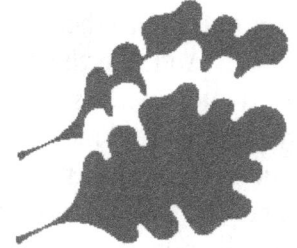

CHAPTER 11 – SUPPORT YOUR LOCAL SHERIFF

A major function and responsibility of any government, whether Federal or State or Local, is to provide for the safety and protection of its citizens. Fair Oaks Ranch officials subscribed to this responsibility as one of their first actions when establishing the City's mission and setting priorities. As described in Chapter 9, the mission included a specific reference to *'provide security, public safety, and police services for the maintenance of good order and the protection of personal and real property located within the City limits'*. Included in the priorities were two separate items dealing with this facet of the government's obligation:

- Contract with a law enforcement agency at a

> reasonable cost for the security of the citizens and the protection of personal and real property within the City limits.
>
> - Provide for reliable fire protection services through arrangement with existing fire protection agencies.

The initial step taken at the first City Council meeting was to appoint a Town Marshall who would serve until appropriate steps could be completed that would provide for a more comprehensive armed enforcement presence within the City. Don Zook, a retired San Antonio police lieutenant, was selected for the Marshall position because of his experience and past law enforcement positions held. His duties were short lived, however, as the Council immediately pursued a contract with the Bexar County Precinct 2 Constable's Office which took effect in April, 1988, only three months after the City's formation. Details on that contract are contained in Chapter Eight. Another less pleasant activity interrupted Zook's term as Town Marshall. His home burned to the ground and required his full time attention while rebuilding. His is only one of three houses to completely burn in the twenty-five years since the City was founded.

What was most unique about the contract with the Constable and evidence of the trust and character of both parties was the fact that it was merely an oral agreement. No documents changed hands. A simple handshake between the Mayor and the Constable made it happen. And it would remain happening for more than a year.

The contract with the Constable provided for the presence of a fully commissioned police officer within the City of Fair Oaks Ranch, including the security area, 24 hours a day in a patrol car. The officer operated with the full support of the City in all three of the counties and had the authority equivalent to an established police force.[1]

The Constable's duties involved responding to calls and patrolling the City streets. Most of the calls were minor in nature as the City remained relatively crime free and void of any serious wrongful activity. For instance, of 29 calls answered in the late spring of 1988, all but two regarded issues such as open doors and windows, false burglar alarms, and damaged or found property. During the same period, 6,654 miles were driven in support of the service.[1]

The Constabulary officers who were on duty in the City drove their own vehicles and received an allowance from the City for that practice. It became evident within a few months that this approach was inconsistent with the low cost priority of the City mission and the City requested bids for the purchase of its first police vehicle. Once the requisite modifications were completed, the vehicle was put into use in late 1988/early 1989 at a substantial savings to the budget as mentioned earlier.

The process worked well for over another year. The community had one of the lowest crime or vandalism rates in the State as evidenced by the types of activities the officers were involved in. Fair Oaks Ranch was the quiet little Camelot that everyone wanted it to be.

As seems always to be the case once a government official

Chapter 11   History Of Fair Oaks Ranch

becomes aware of something that doesn't fit that official's idea of what is right, the handshake arrangement with the Constable ended up in the crosshairs of Bexar County's budget process. In the summer of 1989 Bexar County proposed a written contract that it was believed would be more in line with the operations of both entities and more legally appropriate for the agreement. The trusted handshake arrangement was, in the government's view, not appropriate.

It became apparent, however, that costs associated with a new, written contract with Bexar County for using Constables for our police support would escalate more than desired. Additionally, administrative issues involved with the execution of the contract made the continuation of this approach less than satisfactory.[2] The City was not yet in a position to establish its own police operation and the unacceptability of the Bexar County approach presented the City with a dilemma.

The solution was found in discussions with the Kendall County Sheriff's office on the possibility of enlisting their support. It was an appealing arrangement much like what had worked with the Constable and by October 1, 1989, the discussions resulted in a contract that provided for four new deputies who would use the City's cars, be present in the City 24 hours a day, and be dispatched by the sheriff's office. The contract also provided a savings of $34,000 dollars annually over the already low cost associated with the Constable arrangement. The Constabulary support had been good and provided a much needed service as the City moved through its growing pains. But it was now time to move to the next step.[3] However, not everyone thought it was a good idea to use the

Kendall County Sheriff for police service in Fair Oaks Ranch. Even though the four new officers and their cars and equipment would be paid for by the City, some disagreed with the action. In particular, Kendall County resident Cliff Bruce told the County Commissioners and the Sheriff that there were legal questions concerning the contract. It's not certain what those legal issues were and they must have been minor as this challenge was quickly settled with the presentation of papers showing several attorneys had reviewed the contract and even the Texas attorney general office had approved it.[4] Once again the foresight the Council exercised on all issues of the young city proved prescient.

All was well in Camelot for the next three years. The contract with the Kendall County Sheriff and the performance of the officers was successful and residents and city officials enjoyed a period of significant cooperation. There continued to be little crime or disturbances and residents lived the good life in the City free from San Antonio annexation and free to pursue their own goals. The presence of the officers was often stealth-like but they were in the City and patrolling 24 hours a day.

In the summer of 1992 the Council voted on a motion to approach the Boerne Police Department to take over the police protection services the Sheriff had been satisfactorily providing.[5] This action would involve a two year contract. The move was part of the long range goal of eventually creating the City's own police force. By working with an established and experienced city police function the Council believed the experience gained would facilitate the future formation of its own police force. City police operations were significantly different than a sheriff's operations. It seemed to be a good idea.

Yet, before the Boerne City Council could take up the measure, Mayor Gaubatz surprisingly withdrew the request. His constant practice of keeping his ear to the rail and his eyes looking far forward allowed him to learn that a majority of the Boerne City Council members would not support a contract with Fair Oaks Ranch and it was futile to pursue it. The sheriff's contract was due to expire and any failed effort to change the Boerne Council's position would leave the City without appropriate protection and result in ultimate delays in forming the City's own force.

Therefore, when the negotiations with Boerne did not come to fruition, Don Zook, the Town Marshall during the first few months of the City's existence and whose home was now rebuilt, was appointed to head a panel looking into the steps needed to finally create a Fair Oaks Ranch police force in the near future. The move toward its own police department would allow the City to avoid negotiating a contract every two years or so as well as provide for a stable police force presence in the City. Fair Oaks Ranch was on the path to moving from its teenage years into adulthood.

The proposal was presented to the Council and included the continued use of the Kendall Country Sheriff under contract with dispatching provided by the Kendall County dispatcher - an approach that was less expensive than setting up the City's own dispatcher. After a police force was formed the issue of dispatching would be revisited. As of the time of this writing, a contract with the City of Boerne dispatching function is still the least expensive and most effective process. The target for completing the process of forming an autonomous police presence was January 1, 1993, with a police chief being hired three months before that date by October 1, 1992. That Chief would then hire the officers needed to provide a police presence in the City.[5]

As a result, the Kendall County Sheriff was asked to extend his contract with Fair Oaks Ranch until January 1993 to give the City necessary police protection during the formation of its own police force. Sheriff Steve Stevens, the officer in charge of the contract since its inception, agreed to this arrangement which was also supported by Lee D'Spain who was scheduled to replace Stevens as Kendall County Sheriff on October 1st. Stevens also prepared a proposal for Fair Oaks Ranch to use in organizing its own department including an expressed interest in applying for the job as Chief of the new department.[6]

Either there was an overabundance of law enforcement people needing a job or Fair Oaks Ranch was definitely a desirable place to work because over thirty-six resumes were submitted for the new chief's position.[7] Interviews began on September 3, 1992, with Don Zook heading the culling effort. The resulting short list of acceptable and competitive candidates was submitted to the City Council where a unanimous vote in favor of Roy W. Thomas for the position of Chief of Police was cast by the Aldermen. Thomas, 45 years old and a Sergeant with the San Antonio police department, was scheduled to retire from his then current position after 26 years on the force - the day before the new Fair Oaks Police Department would take over patrol and protection responsibilities in the City. The fit seemed perfect.

Chapter 11   History Of Fair Oaks Ranch

And, as it turned out, it was perfect. Roy Thomas, until his recent retirement, was known throughout the City as the City Administrator and the 'go to man' on the staff for all things involving government functions. During his 20 year association with the City, he has served as the Police Chief and City Administrator. He provided a wealth of skills and knowledge for the successful implementation of many programs. His knowledge of Fair Oaks Ranch operations and processes and history is without equal. And his calm approach to all critical and potentially explosive events is legendary.

The new Police Chief completed his interviewing and hiring activities while he was still working for the San Antonio Police Department, working late into the evenings as the deadline approached. The four officers he selected and who were approved by the Council were sworn in and began their duties on schedule on January 1, 1993. Among them was a 20 year veteran of the Boerne Police Department, Henry Hodge, who was destined for a smidgen of notoriety not too long later. He eventually became the first African-American Sheriff in Texas since the reconstruction days back in the 1800s when he ran for and won the election in Kendall County in 1996 and served for two four year terms.

The black and white patrol cars we see now in the City are relative newcomers to the quiet streets of this city. For the longest time the patrol cars were white with green trim so as to present a low profile law enforcement appearance. The official and crisp looking uniforms the officers wear now are also relative newcomers. The officers once wore tan outfits with minimal accoutrements. The effort was to display a friendly approach to law enforcement and it worked well for the first few years of the department's operation. However, with the growth of the population and it's accompaniment of issues to deal with in a rapidly expanding area of coverage that included assisting other police operations in the area, it became necessary to marry the look of authority with the enforcement effort.

Still, 'back then', the cooperative approach, which continues to this day, was one of the major elements of the department's success. For example, in the first year of operation, the officers made 529 vehicle related violations stops. They issued 382 oral and written warnings rather than tickets for a ratio of 2.6 to one. Camelot even had 'nice' policemen. But they were far busier in other areas with 5,000 calls during the year with more than 85,000 miles driven on official business. Compared to the first year of Constable patrols (6,654) this was a significant increase. And with an astounding 4,885, or 73%, of the calls classified as non-criminal, Fair Oaks Ranch was a peaceful place. In fact of the 21 reported burglaries, 18 were construction site or open garage activities.

The successful establishment of a fully functional police department was not the only thing going on during that time. Many other significant activities were taking place that continued to enhance and improve the quality of life within the City limits. It is not the intent of this book to cover them all. But day by day the volunteers who assisted the Mayor and the Council were critical to everything coming together and were always doing yeoman's work that benefits all of us today.

Not all things worked out so well as the establishment of a

Chapter 11

police force and that is the subject of the next chapter. It is a subject near and dear (pun intended) to everyone who lives here. The passion is evident in all discussions about the subject and no one I know of is exempt. There seems to be no subject less controversial or more contentious.

That subject is – DEER.

CHAPTER 12 – OH MY DEAR

Deer in Fair Oaks Ranch is a subject of endless discussion and cussin' to everyone who lives here. The passion is evident in all dialog about the subject and no one is exempt. There are no right answers to the issue nor are there any wrong answers. The limited variety of solutions conflict with each other on almost a daily basis somewhere in the City. The subject seems unresolvable and over the entire life of the City no one has successfully reached consensus on the right direction to take.

So the problem, or as some would believe, the blessing, continues without end.

The deer in discussion is mainly Odocoileus virginianus -

Chapter 12 — History Of Fair Oaks Ranch

known commonly as the Whitetail Deer. There are Axis deer in the City as well that wander throughout the City but they don't seem to be as bothersome as the whitetails. They are mainly grass eaters and rarely infringe on a homeowner's prized landscape. They are also more timid, having been the target of hunters year 'round [they are not protected as they are exotic imports which is another story] and flee rapidly at the first sign of human activity in the area. Whitetails are a different thing and the debate has raged for the entire length of the City's existence. It is safe to say that the debate will continue long into the future.

Whitetail deer have been on this continent for millions of years and spent their early days near the Arctic Circle in what is now Canada. About four million years ago they migrated to what we now call the United States.[1] The deer provided early settlers from Europe a means of survival with both food and fur and thus suffered significant swings in population for nearly two centuries.

The fur trade in the early 1800s resulted in more than 5 million deer killed each year. When the fur trade declined the deer populations recovered because of the loss of hunting pressure as well as an increase in deer favorable habitat. As we have learned, habitat is critical to any wildlife survival success. Contrary to Hollywood folklore, whitetail deer do not like the deep, denizens of a mature forest. They are edge dwellers who live in the strips of land that border the forest and give way to meadows where forbs, the favorite deer food, is abundant. And as the increasing human population in the United States cleared more and more of the old growth forests, more and more areas of forb infested land became available for the deer to use.

Unfortunately, for the whitetail deer at least, market hunting in the late 1800s took an even bigger number of these beautiful/hateful animals [depending on your point of view] than the fur trade had. The estimated number of deer left in the entire country at the turn of the 20th century was 500,000 and deer had been extirpated in some areas. Compare this to the current estimated population of deer in Texas alone at over 4 million in 2004 and one can see how serious the deer's decline had become. And one can see how remarkable their recovery has been when you consider that, again in Texas alone, hunters harvest nearly 437,000 deer in a year.[3]

It was the Lacy Act of 1900 that prohibited the interstate trafficking of venison and other wild game that provided the basis for the whitetail deer population to begin its recovery. Now, a little over one hundred years later, whitetail deer are the most widespread deer in the world with over 11 million hunters each year searching for one or more of the 20-25 million animals that now live among us.[1]

The impact of the whitetail deer on the desirability of Fair Oaks Ranch as a place to live is evident in the advertising brochures of the developer and the country atmosphere touted as a prime reason to purchase land north of San Antonio. A

Chapter 12 History Of Fair Oaks Ranch

little piece of land in the country remains a strong draw for many. But the reality of the situation is that Fair Oaks Ranch has evolved from a scattering of two to ten acre plots to a mixture of garden homes, golf course mini-homes, and a large number of smaller 1-2 acre properties. With this growth it was inevitable for the conflict with the whitetail deer to arise.

To the deer's credit they have been exceptionally adept at adjusting to the changing conditions and actually thrive amidst the controversy. In fact, they have mastered the ability to survive and grow in numbers almost anywhere there is water and their kind of food. They even do quite well when their choice food is not available. The growth of the City and the increasing numbers and variety of plants in all the new landscapes is a perfect setting for these animals. As a result the herd has grown into a significant presence - everywhere.

Earlier in this book we described the area including Fair Oaks Ranch as part of the ecological region called the Edwards Plateau also known as the "Texas Hill Country". This region is also known as one of the best-known deer producing areas in the world.[2] Fair Oaks Ranch is smack dab in the middle of one of the best whitetail deer habitats. They like to live here as much as we do.

As nearly every resident knows, even those few who live behind high fenced, gated areas for good reason, whitetail deer find the homeowner's expensive landscaping delightful. They gorge themselves on the luscious plants the homeowners have carefully planted and mulched and fertilized. More than a few homeowners have planted 'deer resistant' plants and watched them grow and provide a false sense of success. But one morning these same homeowners walk out front to get the paper and discover all those 'resistant' plants gone, their stubby shoots standing erect near the ground or the undeveloped roots resting exposed on the ground next to the hole in the ground where they used to live.

It is precisely this habit of the deer that created the ongoing debate of what to do about it. And the City's involvement began in April 1992, a mere four years after its founding. In response to a non-structured survey collecting input on the issues of most importance to the citizens, 20% of the comments were directly related to deer management.[4] The City had limited authority over the deer since the animals are managed by the State of Texas. Therefore, the Council took on the responsibility of contacting the Texas Parks and Wildlife Department for assistance.

Unfortunately, there was to be little progress for two reasons:

- First, since the deer are the property of the State of Texas [managed by the State as they like to say], the City has no authority to act unilaterally in resolving its problem;

- Second, there was no consensus in the City that the problem *was* a problem. Half the residents wanted to keep the deer at whatever cost and half wanted to completely extirpate them at whatever cost.

It was, and continues today, a typical quandary.

So the issue simmered under the radar for an astonishing eight years while the deer population within the City grew to a herd of approximately 2,500 to 3,000.[5] State biologists thought there were only about 1,000 deer but a survey conducted in 2001 showed that estimated number to be alarmingly low. Complaints about the deer continued and even grew in number. Incidents involving deer, according to police reports, were increasing with nearly 8 deer/auto collisions a month in 1999.[7]

The Council's approach to almost every contentious issue was to search for consensus. The mission of the City and the commitment of its leaders to involve the residents in major decisions was a significant factor in the formation of the first deer committee in March 1992. The committee involved a broad cross section of experts and citizens with a report due to the Council by June of that year.

It was to be discovered, as has been the result time and time again over the years, that there was no hope of reaching consensus in the three months allocated for the committee's efforts. As will become evident, the committee remained an important part of the search for a solution for at least two years – more than eight times longer than planned.

One of the first things the Committee did was develop a series of deer education articles to be included with the periodic Mayor's newsletter. A questionnaire was also prepared and distributed to the residents of which 856 were returned. Of those that were returned, 70% believed there was a deer problem in the City. Armed with that information and confident that a solution was within reach, the Committee embarked on a bold plan that included the trapping and relocating of more than 200 deer. That first effort took place in November 1993 and the deer that fell to the trapper's net were used to repopulate an area in Mexico that had suffered the loss of most of it herd of white-tails.

Fast forward to the turn of the century when the subject of trapping was once again on the table. By happenstance this effort involved the City of Lakeway on the shores of Lake Travis north of Fair Oaks Ranch and west of Austin. Lakeway had a deer problem equal or even greater than Fair Oaks Ranch. According to an article in the San Antonio Express News on July 7, 2000, by Ron Henry Strait, Lakeway's sanitation crews removed 700 deer carcasses in 1998, most resulting from collisions with autos. Lakeway also trapped and removed 650 deer at a cost of $65,000.[6] It doesn't take much calculating to determine that if Fair Oaks Ranch were to trap and remove enough of their three thousand deer population to reach the desired population of 500 that the $250,000 cost was prohibitive.

But the prevailing feeling was that a little bit would at least help. And Lakeway was about to embark on another trapping effort with a target of 1,000 deer. This effort was sanctioned by the Texas Parks and Wildlife Department (TPWD) and funded by Mexico and the State of Nuevo Leon at a cost of about $100,000. The problem for Lakeway was that the target was later increased to 1,400 deer and Lakeway couldn't meet that target without outside help. Because of the ongoing study relative to methods to reduce its own deer population, Fair Oaks Ranch was the obvious place to get help. As a result of all this maneuvering, the City became a deer trapper almost by default.

The trapping was to take place between December 2001 and

March 2002 – almost ten years after the first deer committee held its first meeting. Because of the need for immediate action in response to the Lakeway crisis, the Mayor was forced, much to his chagrin, to renege on a promise he had made in July 2001. He had then pledged, in support of open and consensus government, that he and "the City Council, and the [newly formed] Deer Management Committee…will keep you informed and…take no action without special newsletters and Town Hall Meetings."[8]

Throughout this same time, the City and the Deer Management Committee were actively supporting an effort by State Representative Harvey Hildebran to permit cities to declare a health and safety hazard if needed, an authority then retained at the county level of government. This effort resulted in House Bill 1427 that would allow a political subdivision to trap, transport, and transplant whitetail deer without obtaining a permit or license from Texas Parks and Wildlife.[9] Unfortunately, although the bill made it out of committee favorably, it did not progress any further and those cities whose deer problems gave rise to the bill were back to square one.

The trapping effort of 2001/2 began as scheduled but did not proceed without incident. Some of the residents who favored the whitetail deer in any number within the City gathered near the trapping locations to voice their objections to the "cruel and inhumane" actions being taken by the authority of the City. It was the first protest activity in the City and signaled the emotions involved in protecting the deer. One protester even claimed to have witnessed the exposed bone of a compound fractured leg of a deer caught under the netting and struggling to free itself. This claim became an issue at a council meeting with assertions of inhumane activity but the alleged bone was later proven to be only a buck's antler and not a broken bone.

Trapping deer is not like using the simple catch and release traps many residents are familiar with in handling the ubiquitous raccoons and hard to trap armadillos and other vermin that roam freely throughout the City. Deer are not interested in coming close to a human, excluding those few some of the residents have tamed. And their hoofs are sharp. And their ability to use them is something to behold. As Linda Zartler, City Secretary at the time of the first trapping in 1993 and enlisted to physically help 'manage' the deer once under the net, said: "I was assigned to 'comfort' the deer as they could easily stress out from the trapping. I would hold them down under the netting, in an attempt to keep them from tangling their antlers or hooves any more than necessary in the netting. In some cases dropping the net would cover 15-20 deer at one time, so many people were involved and it was done as quickly as possible to ease the stress on the animals."

The 2002 trapping resulted in 212 deer being caught and transported to the border between Texas and Mexico where bureaucratic red tape and inept bungling, inept local authorities, and inept rules created onerous delays in the movement of the deer and the loss of some of the animals in the process. Although technically a success, the trapping effort was a strong example of how difficult it is to control whitetail deer populations in a non-lethal manner. It was a strong lesson for the Deer Management Committee and the City Council. It was also evident that Fair Oaks Ranch needed to find a more humane and permanent solution.

Another trapping was urged by a number of residents but the City did not pursue it for two reasons:

- First, the experiences of the first effort and its associated expense argued convincingly against the effort.

- Second, the TPWD had changed its rules to require that Chronic Waste Disease be proven non-existent in the population being trapped. Chronic Wasting Disease (CWD) is a transmissible neurological disease of deer and elk that produces small lesions in brains of infected animals. It is characterized by loss of body condition, behavioral abnormalities and death.[10] The new rules required the trapping and killing of at least 10% of the target population for testing before trapping approval could be granted. The cost and restrictive rules that allow only relocation to in-state locations made the process unreasonable.[11]

Nothing rarely resolves itself without some sort of external influence, especially where survival of the fittest applies. And in Fair Oaks Ranch the fittest were the best fed deer in the area. Therefore, it is understandable that in the spring of 2010 the deer situation once again raised its undesirable head like a deer does when you approach it unexpectedly.

The deer population had continued its growth unabated. The animals expanded their damaging foraging for nearly eight more years and the resident complaints rose in number along with the burgeoning deer population. It was dêja vous all over again. In response, the City Council hoped for some new solutions that technology or experience may have created and might be available. What better way to find out than forming a committee?

Welcome the new deer management committee labeled the Deer Ad-Hoc Advisory Committee. In January 2010 by Resolution 141 the City Council authorized this committee. The mission, plainly stated in the resolution, included: gathering, preparing, and presenting an in-depth report on information received from Texas Parks and Wildlife representatives on deer and their natural habitats, examining and outlining deer management options including associated costs, developing new routes for an annual deer census count, and providing an assessment of deer population impact over the next 5-10 years.

This may sound like kicking the can down the road one more time, but in all fairness there are not a lot of other options. Although this effort may sound eerily familiar to the first committees' approach, this one included a broader approach involving more agencies and expanding the search for more technological solutions. It was also the first time the Texas Parks and Wildlife Department had authorized this type of study for an urban/rural area.

The committee's responsibility to recommend options for deer management are in full swing beginning with the November 2011 City Council authorization for a research contract that was to trap and tag 300-400 deer to monitor their movements, obtain a more accurate census of the population, and determine if contraception would be a viable option.[12] Some of

Chapter 12   History Of Fair Oaks Ranch

those deer visit me from time to time in my front yard sporting their ear tags or radio collars.

A question is imperative here: If the research determines there are too many deer in Fair Oaks Ranch [as we already know] and their migratory habits don't indicate they stray far from home [as we already know] and there are no processes available to the City to deal with the problem [as we already know] …what's the only proven answer? There are a number of people in the City who would be willing to volunteer the only certain solution and the activity involved with that solution.

Unfortunately, as they say, that ain't gonna happen any time soon.

And so the saga continues as this current experiment is underway. If history is a precursor to the future, Fair Oaks Ranch will be dealing with the whitetail deer issue long after this Camelot that is too far from the City of San Antonio to be of an interest to anyone is surrounded by the urban development already underway to the south. The City's now confined deer population will probably be the subject of many conversations and City action for a long time to come. Ask the City of Hollywood Park, surrounded by San Antonio, if you want to know those kinds of details. You will get an earful for sure.

If you do ask the question, you are likely to get a response similar to the satirical letter to the editor of the Fair Oaks Gazette written by Major "Big Daddy" Buck. Major Buck shares his unhappiness with the does wearing ear rings with bright colors and numbers and thinks that the does visiting San Antonio, since it has moved so close, are becoming 'citified'. He says he may have to leave the City and move west but his son Minor Buck believes everything is alright and the does are just being cool. He likes the way things are going.[13]

He's probably right. Citified or old fashioned – the whitetail deer will always be a force to reckon with.

Chapter 12　　　　　　　History Of Fair Oaks Ranch

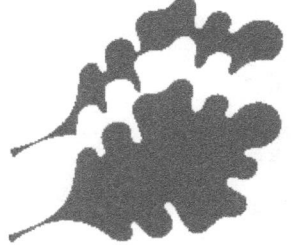

CHAPTER 13 - BRIDGE OVER TROUBLED WATERS

The search for the migratory routes of the deer is not the first of such searches on Fair Oaks Ranch. During the fledgling days of the City, a serious problem with normal traffic flow as well as a serious safety concern became evident. Resolutions to these two significant problems required a concerted effort that was taken up immediately.

The natural dividing line in the City is the Cibolo Creek as it runs from the west to the east and bisects the City into two nearly equal segments. This dividing line was used as the boundary between Fair Oaks North and Fair Oaks South during the formation of the City as it exists today and discussed earlier. While this division of the City was a necessary adjunct to the combination of the two segments, it brought into play a feeling, over time and with the help of a few natural phenomena, that the northern section was getting short shrift in many areas of city services. The first road maintenance plan had scheduled work on the northern roads way down the list while many southern roads received attention. The fact that the southern roads were more heavily used and thus more in need of repair at the beginning of the maintenance plan was small comfort for the northern residents.

But it was natural events that brought it all into focus and spurred the Council and the Mayor to change priorities; not because of the road maintenance issue but for a much more serious concern.

South Central Texas is an area that is most prone to flooding during those periods of heavy rains that come to the area between the well-known droughts. Whereas most areas in the country receive their rainfall in bouts of showers over a number of days, South Central Texas is well known for its thunderstorms with heavy deluges that come quickly and blast through the Hill Country with uncommon strength.

Known by many as Flash Flood Alley, the Hill Country provides an ideal geological foundation for heavy rains. Pacific moisture flows in from the west and collides with Gulf/Atlantic moisture from the southeast. A simple trigger can start the process and the storms flow rapidly from the southwest to the northeast along the opposing moisture systems that are fed continually by large masses of water vapor.

Major flooding as a result of these conditions is commonplace with just a few in the era of Fair Oaks Ranch development listed here:[1]

August 1 – 4, 1978: Rain initiated by the remnants of Tropical Storm Amelia fell over Central Texas with rainfall totaling more than 48 inches near Medina in Bandera County establishing a U.S. record of extreme point rainfall for a 72-hour period. Major flooding occurred on the Medina and Guadalupe Rivers. Thirty-three lives were lost and total damages reportedly exceeded $110 million.

June 4, 1986: San Antonio reported 6.5 inches during 24 hours. Other unofficial amounts of about 10 inches caused widespread flash flooding. Subsequent river flooding lasted for several days along Medina and San Antonio Rivers. Local damage was estimated at $3 million.

July 16 – 17, 1987: During the evening of July 16th and early morning of July 17th, storms produced flash floods across seven counties north and northwest of San Antonio. Flooding caused tragic loss of life when a church bus filled with 39 teenagers and 4 adults was swept into a raging river. Ten persons drowned and the remaining 33 were rescued by helicopter.

May 5, 1993: Up to 8 inches of rainfall in Bexar County produced large peaks on Olmos Creek and Salado Creek.

October 17 – 18, 1998: Up to 30 inches of rainfall occurred

Chapter 13   History Of Fair Oaks Ranch

in a two-day period. Thirteen stream flow-gauging stations in the Guadalupe and San Antonio River Basins recorded peak discharges equal to or greater than the 100-year peak and record-breaking peak discharges were recorded at 11 of the stations. Thirty-two lives were lost and property damage was estimated to be $500 million.

June 30 – July 7, 2002: As much as 35 inches of rain fell during this eight-day storm event. The heaviest depths occurred in the Texas Hill Country northwest of San Antonio, with flooding affecting about 80 counties in Texas. Record flood stages occurred at sites on the Medina River, San Antonio River, Sabinal River and Nueces River. The floods caused 12 deaths and damage to about 48,000 homes, with total damages totaling close to $1 billion. Nearly 250 flood rescue calls were reported, more than 130 roads were closed and thousands of homes and businesses lost electrical power and telephone service.

Everything about Texas is big including its ranking in number of fatalities due to flooding. The top sixteen flash flood/flood fatality States by number of fatalities from 1960 to 1995 shows Texas garnering first place in this not so pleasant category.[2]

1. Texas - 612
2. California - 255
3. South Dakota - 248
4. Virginia - 241
5. West Virginia - 240
6. Pennsylvania 188
7. Mississippi - 181

8. Colorado - 168
9. Louisiana - 149
10. Missouri - 122
11. Georgia - 112
12. New York - 107
13. Ohio - 102
14. Arizona - 96
15. Kentucky - 93
16. Tennessee - 91

Not included in the reports of flooding in Bexar County is the rainfall the City received on June 22, 1991. On that day more than seven inches of rain fell during a one and one half hour period causing wide spread flooding in the City. Power was out up to eleven hours. Water mains broke. Numerous alarm systems were triggered. But most importantly flooding on the Cibolo Creek crossing on Ralph Fair Road, effectively cut off all transportation on the road.

Under these circumstances, the City of Fair Oaks Ranch was literally broken in two. The northern resident's only way to reach southern destinations was to ride north on Ralph Fair

Road to SH 46 then into Boerne and IH 10. Travel along Amman Road into Boerne, the only other way, was impossible because of the low water crossings on that road that were also flooded. These kinds of conditions had happened in the prior years' floods. But now there was a

government whose job it was to provide security and safety to its residents and look into fixing these problems.

Two major aspects of this isolation of the north became very apparent in short order. First, there was no way to ensure rapid response to medical emergencies during times of flooding. Second, there was no way to provide fire suppression services during the same time. Both the emergency response teams and the fire department equipment were located in the south section of the City. Something needed to be done and it needed correction in as soon a time frame as possible.

Although the fire department solution was the least difficult and proceeded with little controversy, it would not be completed until October of 1999. A major issue was the availability of land on which to place a fire station. There was little available real estate that would fill the needs of the northern part of the City and funds were limited as well. It was becoming an almost impossible task.

Once again, however, the Fair family came to the rescue by donating a 2.5 acre parcel for the City's use.[3] This parcel became available almost serendipitously because of TXDOT work on Ralph Fair Road. When the City was formed, Ralph Fair Road followed a line north past the Cibolo Creek crossing to a point where it made a 90 degree right turn to the east. The state of Texas improved the shoulders of Ralph Fair Road and during that project created the gently rounded turn in the road between Silver Spur Road and Meadow Creek Trail. This action left a triangular section of property with little to no use to anyone – except the volunteer fire department.

The Council had been looking for property since the 1991 flood. With the land donated, the Council accepted bids for a new fire station for the northern section of the City in this triangular piece of property. The station could provide service to the north in all weather conditions and provide or receive assistance in cooperation with the Boerne Fire Department when needed.

The Cibolo Creek crossing was a more immediate project. And while the effort was on-going to find land for the fire station work also was underway to resolve the Cibolo Creek issue. The first problem was that the City had no authority to do anything about the low water crossing on the Bexar County and Comal County line. Another factor that rendered a solution unreachable even if the authority had existed was funding. Additionally, the creek flooded only sporadically with unusually heavy rainfall. With normal rainfall the caves beneath the creek bed allowed most of the water to flow beneath the surface in the area rendering the creek deceptively dry after normal rains but a raging flood during the heavier rains. There was no way around the problem of limited access to the north during heavy rainfall except a higher bridge.

Not that easy. Bridges are notoriously expensive to build and the road was a state asset and anything concerning bridges on a state asset was a state activity. Therefore, in their usual spirit of cooperation, the Council and the Fair Oaks Ranch Homeowners Association joined hands and approached the TXDOT for assistance in upgrading the Cibolo Creek crossing.

Chapter 13   History Of Fair Oaks Ranch

By May of 1992, less than a year after the flooding that started the process, Mayor Gaubatz reached an agreement with the Texas Transportation Commission to build a $450,000 bridge to replace the low water crossing at Cibolo Creek on FM 3351, Ralph Fair Road. Many people were involved in this effort including the Fair Oaks Ranch Homeowners Association, the City Council, State Representatives, and a Kendall County Judge.[4]

It was designed to handle 25 times more water than the old drainage culvert. A preconstruction meeting was held on July 21, 1994. All environmental and other problems were resolved. The road would soon be open at all times except for pesky ten year floods. And there was no cost to the City. It was a win – win for everyone.

By the summer of 1995 the bridge was complete. And guess what? As nature would have it, three years later the ten year rainfall and flooding that was predicted would exceed the new bridge's increased capacity actually occurred. This was the first time the Cibolo Creek halted traffic on Ralph Fair Road since the bridge was built.

Subsequent closings during each ten year flooding cycle have shown that there may be a need for an even higher bridge, especially with the growth occurring north of the Cibolo Creek and the increased traffic flow. Preliminary dialogue with TXDOT is in progress as of this writing.

PART FOUR

FAMILY FEUDS

Every family has its times of dissension and Fair Oaks Ranch in its teenage years was not exempt. The exceptional growth and the influx of a significant number of new residents created a few situations where the government trying to do its best job and the interests of the citizens did not always agree. Part Four is focused on only a few of the issues that cascaded into a category of contentiousness.

It is another example of how properly managed government activity can result in resolutions that don't create enemies in the process. There were numerous situations that could have resulted in a breech of trust and confidence. Credit belongs to the involvement of the citizens and their willingness to express their desires and their effort to understand the complexities of the issues for the satisfactory resolution of many conflicts.

As previous mentioned, these few examples of the conflict and cooperation are only a few of the more significant during this period.

Part Four   History Of Fair Oaks Ranch

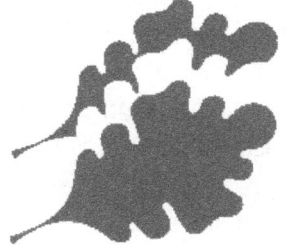

CHAPTER 14 – MOVIN' ON UP TO THE EAST SIDE

Building bridges on a road is child's play compared to getting city facilities approved and in place. It took just two years from first idea to completion of a half million dollar bridge on Ralph Fair Road. By contrast it took almost nine years for the plans of the City's administrative and maintenance complex to see the light of day.

The City's first offices consisted of three rooms in the business building at the intersection of Fair Oaks Parkway and Dietz Elkhorn Road. Two of these leased rooms were on the second floor and served as storage space and a small office for private meetings and other activities. Because of laws governing access to city facilities for handicapped individuals, these two rooms were of limited use to the public.

The third room was on the ground floor and served as a multifunctional office of broad and varied uses. For example, the room housed Linda Zartler (City Secretary) and Debbie Mergele (a part time clerk who doubled as the Deputy Municipal Clerk). This single room also functioned as the City Council's office, official records storage area, and meeting place. The space also served as the reception area for all citizens and guests as well as the offices for police coordination, animal control, building permits, court payments, information center, contractor services, and general area for other governmental officials from various entities to gather and confer.[1] Needless to say, it was a very busy office with little room to maneuver or carry out official business.

In addition to these three rooms, the City also owned the fire station across from the country club and leased the old milk barn off Dietz-Elkhorn Road near No Le Hace for maintenance activities. The fire station had been given to the City by the Fair Oaks Ranch Homeowners Association who had received it as a gift from Ralph E. Fair, Inc.

As the City continued its growth during the two years since its founding it became evident that the administrative and maintenance facilities were not suitable for sustained use. Consequently, a long range study was completed that looked at three alternatives:

> - A one campus approach involving the purchase of 3-5 acres around the fire station. This option was not recommended due to its proximity to then

on-going development of home sites so near the proposed site.

- A three campus approach involving the purchase of the two story building where the three rooms were leased, leaving maintenance in the milk barn, and leaving the fire station alone. This option was also not recommended as it would split up the City's functions over a wide area.

- A three campus approach involving the purchase of three acres adjacent to the building that housed the three offices, construct a 3000 square foot office building to house the City offices and the Fair Oaks Ranch Homeowners Association, and set up police offices in the fire station – then occupied by the Homeowners Association.

This third option was pursued and priced out at $300,000. The design allowed for additional units should the need for space arise. Drawings were created and an informational campaign implemented to advise the citizens of what was being discussed and considered. Since the City did not have the money to pay for the new facilities outright, a bond issue would have to be voted on before any concrete decisions could be made.[2]

Using the Mayor's then commonplace newsletter approach to keeping all citizens in the loop, the Mayor and Council outlined the need for new facilities and the costs of the bond. Designs were completed and public hearings held with a vote scheduled for May 1991. Fair Oaks Ranch was about to earn its right to be called a full-fledged city with modern facilities.

Then – the bond issue was defeated by a 2 to 1 margin.[3] And it was back to the drawing board for the Mayor and the Council. There were a number of citizens who felt we didn't need to be spending $300,000 on facilities so early in the City's life. According to one Alderman who worked almost daily in the cramped quarters of the small office: "Apparently they have forgotten what it was like in the womb."

The City still needed the facilities for proper operation of its functions. But now there would have to be another approach. The problem was that there were no other viable options apparent at the time. So the Council rolled up their sleeves and began looking for a solution that may have been overlooked.

Throughout the formation of the City and continuing through the early years of growth in the City, one person was always present at every council meeting and was actively involved in making certain the City retained its enticing character. That person was Bob Weiss, President of Ralph E. Fair, Inc. His cooperation with the City is legendary and is solely responsible for the inclusion of unincorporated portions confined within the City's border through annexation requests. Without his involvement, the City's authority to mandatorily annex those portions that were required to be excluded in the City's bid for incorporation was limited. Furthermore, the City's character did not support forcing annexation even when authorized.

Over the next few months after the bond's defeat, Bob Weiss watched and listened to the Council's frustration as they tried to discover a solution that would fit in the City's budget and still provide the facilities needed. They were not making much headway and there seemed to be no easy way to achieve their goal.

Many successful people often talk of having a mentor or guardian angel help them work their way through difficult times. When all looks about to fail, these mentors appear out of nowhere and show the way to the successful completion of whatever was about to fall apart. The City of Fair Oaks Ranch had such a guardian angel from the very beginning and that mentor came to the rescue when it looked as if there was no way to resolve the need for adequate office space.

In the spring of 1992, Ralph E. Fair, Inc., represented by Bob Weiss, made an offer to the City of six acres and three buildings at 7286 Dietz Elkhorn for $75,720. The parcel included the maintenance barn then under lease for equipment and supplies. It was a fortuitous event and displayed the continuing positive relationship between Ralph Fair, Jr., Bob Weiss, and the City. A unanimous vote by the Council and broad support for the purchase by the citizens[4] resulted in the rapid conclusion of the purchase.

After minor renovations, the City was able to move into these new facilities by October 1992. The three building complex housed

Chapter 14　　　　　　　History Of Fair Oaks Ranch

all city business and Fair Oaks Ranch Homeowners Association activities in a one stop shopping atmosphere. The City administrative and Homeowners Association functions were carried out in the largest of the two residential buildings - the one closest to Dietz Elkhorn. The police set up operations in the smaller and one-time ranch supervisor's home. Maintenance activities were carried out in the old milk barn.

At that time, the City had two computers that were networked with BNC cables strung through the crawl spaces under the buildings. Over time a third computer was added as a server and cables were run under the driveway between the police office and business office. Adequate space was available for all functions and handicap accessibility laws were finally in force throughout the entire city complex. The Camelot that was a natural part of the rest of the City now included the City offices.

It would be another six years before the City would finally realize its goal of a fully modern and functional business center. But until that time city administrative, police, and maintenance activities were conducted from the modified structures. A clerk was brought on to help with the growing number of duties each ordinance and each new resident created. This employee also functioned as a receptionist to help with the flow of visitors and calls to the offices. Fair Oaks Ranch was becoming more than a new city in rapid order.

For years Mayor Gaubatz wanted to house the City in facilities that advertised the success of the City and the character of the residents. The defeat of the first attempt was disappointing and the stop gap measures of the three outdated buildings was an interim approach. The idea of modern facilities was constantly on his mind and he worked hard to achieve his dream never forgetting for a minute whose city it was.

Then things began to fall in place. In the spring of 1998, the Council approved a plan for three new facilities: an administrative building, maintenance facilities, and a fire station for the north portion of the City.[5] The Mayor's dream was about to come true. This time around there would be no bond issue as the City had built a sufficient reserve of funds to be able to proceed without going into debt. Interestingly enough such action was quite irrelevant as this time there was widespread support for the action. It seems those who had objected to the construction were merely rejecting the issuance of debt. They now agreed that new facilities were needed. It's amazing how much a cash deal can affect outcomes.

Plans were worked over by all the Council members and the staff to ensure everything was covered. Building an office building is like building a house – only with each member of the family wanting his or her own room. The usual glitches occurred, including a technician installing the computer server in the wrong room and the main power breaker box on the

Chapter 14   History Of Fair Oaks Ranch

wrong wall and a few other normal mess ups. All was worked out and the facility came in under budget. All was good with the world.

The new facilities were ready for use by the year 2000. In the process, the Police Department moved into the City's old building and the Fair Oaks Ranch Homeowners Association moved into the Police Department's building – now called the Community Center. A new maintenance building was constructed sometime later with more modern vehicle bays and maintenance repair equipment. These new facilities allowed the growing maintenance department along with the utility operation to complete their varied and increasing duties in a manner befitting those functions.

Fair Oaks Ranch was becoming a mature teenager after surviving its youthful years. It may have been told to go stand in the corner the first time out but it served its time and kept on becoming a personality. The City continued its impressive growth and the services provided by the City continued expanding. Everything was going just fine ... except for a few dark clouds that lingered from the past and were also gathering on the horizon. The rebellion against a fancy building that would have put the City in debt was a tip of the iceberg thing and a minor event. Fair Oaks Ranch was about to enter its first season in the big leagues.

Chapter 14

CHAPTER 15 – BUSINESS AIN'T DOING SO WELL

As the saying goes: It's always something. And Fair Oaks Ranch was no exception. The growth continued unabated even during times of downward housing trends. What the Council, Fair Oaks Ranch Homeowners Association, and scores of volunteers had put together was the envy of many surrounding communities.

It had become enough of a model that Bulverde, Texas, then merely a sprawling area to the east of the City, came to Fair Oaks Ranch for consultation on how to become a city and how to make Bulverde as desirable as Fair Oaks Ranch had become. What once was thought to be a retirement

Chapter 15 — History Of Fair Oaks Ranch

community for people who wanted to play golf every day was becoming a place the younger generations sought after and Bulverde wanted to pattern their move to incorporation after Fair Oaks Ranch's successes.

It is no wonder that the City was on the road to broad popularity. Good schools, good government, low taxes, many services, and a responsive city council. The mission put in place at the beginning was still in effect like a constitution that won't change without appropriate support. Everything was quiet and peaceful at the 'Ranch'.

Yet, it remained relatively unadvertised and that may be one of the secrets of its success as a city. Except for the developer's scattered signs and word of mouth, a traveler going from California to Florida along IH 10 would have no idea that the City existed. There was no Fair Oaks Ranch on the many various maps of the area and no signage on the highway. That would change. But first things first.

The City needed its identity. And what better way than to have its own US Post Office. Good idea – right? Wrong. The inevitable struggle the US Postal Service (USPS) as a conveyor of letters between families and other non-business activities was just picking up steam. The internet was just gaining its foothold on everyday communication and UPS, FedEx, and other carriers were making inroads into the USPS market. The Fair Oaks Ranch Mayor and Council were rebuffed, nicely, but with no 'let us think about it' hope. There would be no post office for Fair Oaks Ranch. Considering the current problems the USPS now faces, it was an understandable response.

History Of Fair Oaks Ranch   Chapter 15

When it became evident that Fair Oaks Ranch would not be allowed its own post office it seemed the City would always be known as Boerne to those who communicated by mail with it residents. To mitigate this possible confusion, the Council authorized the Mayor to negotiate with the Postal Service on a slightly different approach.

The area now included in the City had always shared the 78006 ZIP Code with Boerne and other non-incorporated areas in both Bexar and Kendall counties. But following the Mayor's efforts beginning in January 1994, federal postal authorities relented and granted the City's wish. A new ZIP code was approved for Fair Oaks Ranch and some of the surrounding area effective July 1, 1995. The City had some identity in Zip Code fashion at least since the lion's share of the ZIP Code area lay within the city limits. But there was more. In keeping with the City's desires for more identity, the USPS also approved the use of the name Fair Oaks Ranch on mailing containers destined to locations within the City. The City had everything a post office would provide except a convenient building nearby to conduct postal activities.

There remain many places in the country's mail system that still refer to 78015 as a Boerne address. That is understandable since some of the code's area is outside the City limits and postal databases throw it out as the city for ZIP Code 78015 (Boerne Post Office handles it). Still, slowly and surely more and more users identify 78015 as Fair Oaks Ranch when requested.

As Mayor Gaubatz commented on the approval: "This new ZIP Code will enhance the identity of our city and also is

Chapter 15 History Of Fair Oaks Ranch

established in such a way that our city should not have a split up code in later years."[1]

Quickly following that step toward clear identity, the new version of the official state map included a dot and the name of the City in its rightful place east of IH 10. The inclusion of the City on the map and in the listing with coordinates was a step the Council had pursued for some time. But it was only the second of three steps envisioned when they went after the ZIP code.

The third step is evidenced every time travelers pass exit 546 on IH 10. After considerable negotiations, the TXDOT approved signage on IH 10 and the service road announcing Fair Oaks Ranch as the primary community accessed with this exit.

Fair Oaks Ranch was now in the ZIP code directory, on the maps, and honored with highway signage. With visibility comes challenge however. At the IH 10 entrance to the City there was vacant land on either side of Fair Oaks Parkway. Except for the small bank building on the southwest corner, the area was as rural as it had been from the beginning. At one time there was the stark, steel skeleton of a multi-story building left over from a failed business venture. But otherwise it was scrubby live oaks, ranch-like land, and undeveloped. The only high rise structure other than the steel dragon across the way was the developer's Fair Oaks wooden tower.

In November of 1996, a Dallas developer presented a plan to the City Council on how he wanted to develop the southwest section for retail.[2] Over a period of two months the developer,

Mr. Don Woodbury, described his plans which included a 50,000 square foot anchor retail operation. He did not need to approach the City as the property was within San Antonio's extra-territorial jurisdiction. But his good will gesture had a positive impact on the Council. "Something is going to be built there," Mayor Gaubatz said. "As much as people might want it, the option of nothing is not an option."

Those most opposed to the development were, understandably, the Pfeiffer portion of the City which had just recently been annexed into the City by actions of the residents themselves. In a straw vote they opposed the developer's idea by a 3 to 2 margin. As a result, the Council scheduled a Town Hall Meeting to present the details of the development to other city residents.

The Council was in favor of the development as it presented the most favorable approach to the space and would prevent other, non-coordinated development activities of less desirable traits access to the land. The buildings would be constructed to present a favorable appearance to the entryway to the City and the developer agreed to allow the City to work with him on the restrictions. It seemed a win-win and the Council agreed with the plan and the town hall approach with Councilman Hal Jones stating: "I think what we've got here is a fellow who showed up with a pretty good horse, and we should go down the road with it."

However, it turned out that this issue would not be as easy as it looked at the beginning. More than 200 people turned out for the Town Hall Meeting on March 18, 1997, where they learned that the proposal was for a 120,000 square foot shopping center to be built behind the existing Frost Bank building. The anchor facility of 50,000 square feet would most likely be a grocery store with other retail facilities including restaurants, a video outlet, dry cleaners, and others.

Objections voiced by the attendees at the Town Hall Meeting included the probability of traffic noise, pollution, and lowered property values. There were also concerns of undesirables coming into the City and security lighting impacting the country atmosphere of the City. Mr. Woodbury reiterated that the owners of the project would let the City be involved in writing restrictions and that the project would not include nightclubs, beer joints, or industrial uses.

Of those attending, the majority was in favor of working with the developer in a controlled approach and the Council voted at its next meeting to cautiously work with the developer. Part of the plan would turn Pfeiffer Road into a cul-de-sac and involve the City in traffic studies and restrictions input. It seemed that Fair Oaks Ranch would be blessed with the ability to influence the appearance and functionality of its main entrance in spite of having no real authority in that regard.

Then something happened on the way to the engineering forum. The developer needed to turn Pfeiffer Road into a cul de sac in order to make the anchor store (an Albertsons grocery store that ultimately was built in Leon Springs and became the HEB that is there now) successful. The Pfeiffer residents persisted in their concerns and showed no signs of backing down from their resistance. Finally, in a show of responsiveness to those concerns, the developer decided to abandon his development efforts and, with the reluctant support of the Council, drop the project.

As a result, the City lost its leverage on that area's development. And although the southwest corner remains undeveloped, the northwest corner now boasts what Mr. Woodbury promised he would not install – a bar, pizza parlor, health club, salon, and other retail operations. So turns the wheel of social involvement and the growing pains involved with maturation.

As it also turns out it was not the last contentious development issue to be placed on the Council's plate in these early years of existence. Within a year, another situation arose that would pit residents against each other and the Council in a position of attempted mediation – this time with Ralph E. Fair, Inc.

From the very beginning of the Fair Oaks Ranch development project, Bob Weiss and Don Smith planned a small, professional business center at the southwest corner of Fair Oaks Parkway and Dietz Elkhorn. They envisioned a number of separate buildings nestled in the live oak motts that were scattered in the area. The 20 small buildings would total 50,000 to 55,000 square feet and provide what Weiss described as "garden office and light retail" facilities. This business park was always in the plans for the development and the maps used from the beginning of the Fair Oaks Ranch development effort displayed this in color.

The City's planning committee approved the "concept" pending completion of platting, traffic control, and restrictions. And in the City's normal fashion, the Council hosted a Town Hall Meeting to obtain feedback from the citizens.

The response was immediate and vocal. More than 250 people attended the meeting, some standing and a number of them spilling into the hallway of the Fair Oaks Ranch Country Club where the meeting was held. The case against proceeding with the plan was laid out by a number of residents. Fair Oaks Ranch does not have the population to support what is proposed; the professional services won't be successful; I don't want to wake up every morning to the smell of donuts cooking; and there is plenty of room for business development out by Interstate 10. The main thrust of the comments carried a strong 'no businesses in Camelot' character. There were valid concerns about the traffic that would ensue, the resulting damage to the roads the City would have to repair. But the breaking of implied, but never spoken, promises that this city would remain without commercial development was spurious.

Others complained that the development would ruin the City's country estate quality of life and could be the first step on the slippery slope to strip center businesses. Some even went so far as to hint at possible legal action. Following the meeting, the issue was placed on the agenda of the next council meeting on June 18, 1998, where it was expected the final decision would be made.

Then once again something happened on the way to the engineering forum. Ralph E. Fair, Inc., and Bob Weiss withdrew the request to seek city council approval of the project. Two things of importance about this decision deserve note. First, there never was a requirement that the City approve the project. The property was not within the City limits at the time and therefore not subject to control. The request was consistent with the developer's continuing cooperation with the City in every facet of its operation. Secondly, Ralph E. Fair, Inc., like the previous developer of the land at the IH 10 entrance, was responsive to the will of the people. Both of these actions are indicative of why people like to live in Fair Oaks Ranch.

Both the positive issues involving the establishment of the City's identity and the contentious issues involving commercial development in the City were fundamental in shaping the City's character and proved that small, responsive government is possible. The volunteers serving on the committees and in council positions and in the Homeowners Association positions were committed to making this experiment in limited government work. Based on the City's positive and continued significant growth, they have been successful.

Chapter 15 History Of Fair Oaks Ranch

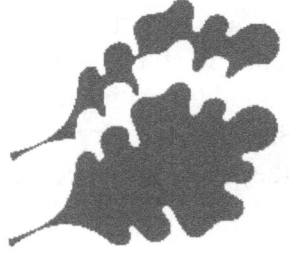

CHAPTER 16 – WATER, WATER, EVERYWHERE

When the northern section of the ranch was developed it was obvious that Ralph E. Fair, Inc. could not afford the resources needed to install a central water system. The lots were too large and the structures built on these lots were separated from each other by distances too great to make running underground piping to each structure feasible. Therefore, each landowner was responsible for drilling his or her own well and installing his or her own septic system.

But when the development effort moved to the southern sections in Bexar County, the closer proximity of the homes to each other allowed for the installation of a central water

Chapter 16   History Of Fair Oaks Ranch

system to each lot. As mentioned earlier, this water system and the water it provided was included in the purchase price of the land. The residents did not have to pay for the water they received or the maintenance of the underground piping systems. It was a win-win for all involved. The owner received a significant benefit and Ralph E. Fair, Inc. was true to its word. Fair Oaks Ranch was gaining a reputation of fairness, commitment to quality, and staying power. The developer was revered for a characteristic uncommon in the industry – honesty; 'my word is my bond' was a reality.

To provide the water to the landowners, Ralph Fair, Jr., formed the company known as Glenpool and drilled wells into what is known as the Trinity River System which flows from Oklahoma to the north and beneath this part of the Hill Country. This system is not as well known as the most famous of the aquifers in these parts: the Edwards Aquifer, a vast underground storage tank that holds uncalculated amounts of clean, potable water. The water in the Edwards Aquifer provides water for a vast area of South Central Texas for both normal consumption and irrigation of water starved crops in the midst of the brutal Texas summers.

The Trinity System, which includes the Glen Rose and Cow Creek Aquifers, differs significantly from the Edwards in that the water is held in the limestone rock and its fissures and cracks as opposed to the Edwards that holds a lion's share of it water in underground caves. It takes a number of wells to produce the water needed for the City of Fair Oaks Ranch and by 1994 there were 38 wells in operation with two more under construction. These wells were capable of producing over 2 million gallons of water a day.

When Ralph Fair, Jr., and Bob Weiss formed Glenpool it was always their intent to sell the company when it was appropriate during the development's life cycle. There would be a time when the development reached full potential that water system should be operated by someone other than the developer. With that in mind and in response to hints from Bob Weiss that sales activity may be forthcoming, the City Council authorized the formation of a Water Supply and Disposal Committee in May 1994. The mission of this committee was to ensure that when the City of Fair Oaks Ranch was fully developed, it would have an adequate, good quality, water supply.

The committee presented its report in March of 1995. Five conclusions were presented at a Town Hall Meeting on March 9, 1995, that ultimately would have a significant impact on water supply management within the City:

- There appears to be an adequate supply for present and future household personal requirements but under severe drought conditions, the water supply for landscaping, swimming pools, and other uses was undetermined.

- A definable and workable conservation plan should be developed and adopted by the City Council.

- The City should commence financial studies to explore the purchase of the Water and Sewer Company.

- Alternate sources of water should be explored as outlined in the geology report and should begin immediately.

- The City should carefully monitor efforts outside the City to create water districts or any other political or environmental initiatives that could affect the control of our water resources.

Water Districts, alternate sources, conservation plans all eventually came to be. But the purchase of the water company was put on a fast track and efforts were begun to determine the feasibility of doing so and the fiduciary appropriateness of the action. Since the sewer functionality was included in the Glenpool operation, any purchase would have to include that operation as well. However, since the sewer system was limited to only a portion of the water system pool of customers, it became a secondary issue. Many residents of the older section received water service but used individual septic systems for their sewer needs.

A major reason for taking some sort of action rested in the publicized intent by Glenpool to go on the market at some time in the future. If the company went on the market and the City was not in the market, a private investment firm could end up owning the water resources and the distribution of that water the City depended on. As the City's mission indicates, this would not be acceptable as there would be no way to ensure that the rates remained as low as possible. The profit motive of a private firm would certainly have an effect on rates whereas the City could operate it in a non-profit status.

The first action needed while the study to determine feasibility was underway was to obtain from Glenpool a letter giving the

City first rights to purchase the water system. This protected the City from losing the system to an outsider without knowledge that a deal was being worked. The consistent integrity and cooperation of the Ralph E. Fair, Inc., and Bob Weiss notwithstanding, it was prudent business to obtain these types of instruments.

Thinking of buying a water company and actually buying one are two vastly different activities. And the Task Force established by the City Council in the spring of 1995 had to plow through myriad tasks to reach even the beginnings of negotiations for the purchase. Not the least of these was the need to ensure broad public support. Concerns over the Fair Oaks Ranch Country Club's use of water had always been a hot topic, especially among newcomers who did not know or understand that the Club's water usage on the golf course was beneficial to the City. Many of them felt the club wasted water keeping the greens 'green' when the rest of the residents' water usage was restricted.

There exists no permit to dispose of effluent from the sewer system, no matter how pure it may be, into the Cibolo Creek. As a result, the club uses the water the sewer system produces for the club's irrigation needs. If there is insufficient effluent for the club's purpose, there are additional City irrigation wells in the Hosston Sligo aquifer that produce saline contaminated water from deep below the Lower Trinity aquifer that does not impact the City's supply.

A number of actions was required to make the purchase possible. As mentioned, public support was a number one item in compliance with the City's mission. An engineering appraisal was needed. Also, a bond under the certificate of obligation authority of the City would be needed if the City was to finance the purchase – the reserve was far too small to help make the action a cash deal. Contracting with a financial advisor was then a required activity to manage the sale of the required bonds. Also the Texas Natural Resources Commission (now known as the TCEQ or Texas Commission on Environmental Quality) would have to grant approval of the sale and purchase after a lengthy public notice process. On top of all this, the City would also have to ramp up its employee base to take over the various functions of the company.

Three years after the first idea of buying the company surfaced, it was time in the usual council approach to things of this nature to get the citizen's final feelings on the issue. A mail-in postcard was sent to the residents asking for their input on the purchase which included a bond offering to fund it. The bond was to be paid for out of proceeds of the water company and not the general fund or taxes. As such, only the users of the water and sewer systems would carry the burden of the bond payments.

A Town Hall Meeting was then held on May 22, 1997, where numerous questions were addressed and the entire plan presented to the attendees. With 75 residents attending, Mayor Gaubatz outlined the sale price of $4.1 million for the complete system which included: 40 wells, 4 water treatment plants, 7 water storage tanks with a capacity of over 2 million gallons, approximately 254,000 feet of water pipes serving over 1,540 metered users, and a complete sewage treatment facility with 700 users. Glenpool would continue to manage the operation for two years while the City came up to speed on the intricacies of how to run a water and sewer company.

The City sent postcards to residents soliciting their input and by May 28, 1997, 835 mail-in postcards had been returned with 821 in favor of the purchase. Citizen support was obvious and the Council then began the actions needed to complete the purchase with a target of October 1, 1997. The TNRC approval process required a period of public notice for objections and when not a single dissenter surfaced they granted approval. That didn't seal the deal however. There were more actions needed. Selection of a firm to sell the bonds was required. And the final action was to obtain approval from the Attorney General of Texas. Fortunately, that was not an issue and the approval was granted in short order.

It was then only a matter of closing the sale. On December 2, 1997, the deal was closed. And as they say, after that it was just water over the dam.

Or was it?

Chapter 16

History Of Fair Oaks Ranch

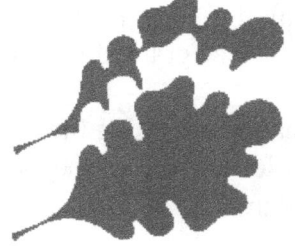

CHAPTER 17 – MAKING WATER FLOW UPHILL

In reality, however, the purchase of the water company from Glenpool was more than just water over the dam. It was to be the start of getting water before it went over the dam. But when it comes to water, there are as many items of confusion as there are stones in a Fair Oaks Ranch front yard. And separating fact from fiction is sometime a difficult exercise.

But first, we must go back in history again to lay the groundwork for what was to happen beginning in the mid-1990s and continuing for nearly ten years. As anyone who lived here during the period 2010 through 2011 can attest it was hot and dry. In fact, it was a dam dry period of unequaled experience. Both the Medina and Canyon Lake reservoirs suffered from extremely low levels. Even if the once considered dam across Cibolo Creek had been built it would still remain a dam dry period.

For those who have lived here for years and experienced other droughts and heat waves, it was just another Texas winter/summer dry spell with a little more punch than usual. For those who were experiencing their first Texas drought and heat wave, it must have seemed like they had moved into the inferno of hell.

The truth of the matter is the summer of 2011 would turn out to be the hottest June through August in Texas on record. That record also surpassed the records of all the other states in this country including the many that were having the same drought issues.[1] Texas is always doing something up big and the heat, combined with the drought, pushed Texas to the top of the list. Oklahoma's 1934 Dust Bowl record had to accept the result that it would slip to third on the list of driest periods for that three month span.[2] The U.S. Drought Monitor reported on August 30, 2011, that over 95% of the state of Texas was in extreme and exceptional drought with more than 81% of the state in the worst category – exceptional.[3]

As mentioned above, this was not the first hot spell or drought and it certainly will not be the last. The entire recorded history of rainfall, or lack thereof, in Texas is rife with alternating periods of droughts and floods. Fair Oaks Ranch is situated between a semi-arid area to the west and a much wetter area to the east. Although the San Antonio area receives, on average, 29 inches of rain each year (some sources say 33 inches), any given year may see only 10 inches while the next year may see more than 50 inches.[4]

The history of droughts in Texas is extensive and according to tree ring studies, droughts as severe or even more severe than the 1957 and the 2011 droughts have occurred even before we began keeping records.[5] Since the first drought recorded in 1870, there have been recurring droughts in 1885-87, 1908-12, 1924-25, 1934-35, 1950-57, 1962, 1965, 1970-72, 1995-96, 1999-2002, 2005-06, 2010-11.[6] Of significance to the observer of detail is the recurrence of droughts so close together over the past fifteen years versus those that occurred earlier in the twentieth century.

In early 1994, seventeen years before the 'worst drought in Texas recorded history' descended on the state, the City of Fair Oaks Ranch began an effort that seems prescient today. The nearest significant drought in the area was more than twenty years in the past. But the Council was concerned about the sustainable supply of water for the growing community.

The Trinity Aquifer system was the City's only supply and with demand at over two million gallons a day during dry times and significant growth projected in the future, the Council approved the formation of a Water Supply and Disposal Committee in the spring of 1994 as mentioned in the previous chapter. The committee's report was due in January 1995[7] - coincidentally the beginning of the 1995-1996 drought. In the meantime, an effort to conserve water through ordinances and voluntary reductions was put in place.

The report was delivered to the Council on time and in the detail desired. The committee members were all volunteers and devoted significant amounts of time in session and individually to produce their recommendations. The

Chapter 17　　　　　　　　　History Of Fair Oaks Ranch

membership of citizen volunteers was composed of:

>   Chairman- Ted Villa
>   Jack Bessellieu
>   Tom Hamilton
>   Hal Jones
>   Don McClelland
>   Seth Mitchell
>   Frank Shipman

The committee presented the five findings previously listed and finding number 4 became the basis of this chapter:

Alternate sources of water should be explored as outlined in the geology report. This work should begin immediately.

All of the remaining initiatives of the committee were forward looking and almost ESP in presentation. At the time of this writing, all the findings and recommendations have proven accurate including the formation of water districts when others in the surrounding area decided to become concerned with the future availability of water.

So, on March 9, 1995, the Mayor hosted a Town Hall Meeting at the Fair Oaks Ranch Country Club to discuss the committee's report.[8] Seventy-five interested citizens attended this meeting to hear about the water company purchase and other items concerning water. After assuring the attendees that there was no water crisis but that the City needed to prepare for the needs of the growing population, the meeting covered many issues: Fair Oaks Ranch was the biggest user of the Trinity Aquifer (likened to a bucket with a hole in it leaking into the Edwards Aquifer) with Boerne a close second. However, Boerne had its lake for an alternate source and it was extremely unlikely that Fair Oaks Ranch could tap into that.[9]

The very first mention that there was a feasible possibility that Fair Oaks Ranch could get Canyon Lake water came out of the report that also included possibilities with the San Antonio Water System and building a dam across Cibolo Creek. The forty million dollar price tag ruled out the dam across the Cibolo almost immediately and the Canyon Lake water rose to the top of the list due to a pipeline to provide water to Bulverde to the east that had just reached the planning stages.

The resulting activity to bring water from a source other than the Trinity Aquifer had its first labor pains at this meeting. It would, in fact, take nearly ten years of birthing labor for it to see the light of day.

The Guadalupe-Blanco River Authority (GBRA) is the organization responsible for the management of the water above and below the Canyon Lake dam. And the Council went to them with a memorandum of agreement for the purchase of water if and when they extended the pipeline from Bulverde to Fair Oaks Ranch and Boerne.[10] It was the first official step in the ten year process that would ultimately be successful in bringing relief to the constant removal of water from the Trinity Aquifer. Dan Kasprowicz, Council Member and Head of the Fair Oaks Ranch Utility Board, suddenly became deeply involved in the water business – more so than he ever thought possible.

Chapter 17 History Of Fair Oaks Ranch

Bureaucracy and planning in governmental activities is not known for rapid progress. Over the next three years those involved in making the water solution a reality worked to design for the future. There were at least fifty meetings with the GBRA over this period that resulted in several plans.[11] One of these plans that held the most promise would deliver eight million gallons of water a day through the pipeline – five million to San Antonio and three million to other buyers, including Fair Oaks Ranch. The ultimate cost would depend on the number of buyers and without San Antonio involved the cost would, of course, escalate.[12]

Finally, an agreement with the San Antonio Water System to buy Canyon Lake water signaled a major step forward. This effort was a separate issue from the Fair Oaks Ranch project. But it was a valuable event that helped the little fish in this proposed stream find an adequate and beneficial flow. The San Antonio Express News weighed in with its editorial support on Friday, September 19, 1997: "The agreement shows city officials – and the region – are finally moving ahead toward a sound future ... another delay would be foolish". [13]

The only thing needed was the approval from the Texas Natural Resource Commission (regularly referred to as simply the TNRC). Slam dunk, as they say. Not so. The first indication there may be problems with proceeding as planned came from the Canyon Lake Water Supply Corporation which wanted to build its own treatment plant. "The people we serve want to own their own plant," Dale Yates, the General Manager, was quoted as saying. "That would allow us to control our own costs and long-term cost would be less."[14] Fortunately, that issue was quickly resolved to everybody's satisfaction. Phew! Ready to roll.

Then in late October 1999, the GBRA Board of Directors approved the water supply contracts for both Fair Oaks Ranch and Boerne. The contracts would run through December 31, 2037 with options for 20 year extensions to 2057 and 2077. Both Boerne and Fair Oaks Ranch would receive approximately 1,120 acre feet of water per year which equated to a little over 1 million gallons per day. Each city reserved a total amount of water of over 1,800 acre-feet for Boerne and 1,400 acre-feet for Fair Oaks Ranch. The Fair Oaks Ranch Council was prepared to authorize the Mayor to sign the contract.[15]

Reserving a supply of water has a special meaning that would end up costing the new water company significant amounts of money. But it was a system that guarantees the City's ownership of future supplies. Consider the reserving process as a sort of retainer fee. GBRA could not sell the water to anyone else as long as the City made timely payments. Once the pipeline was operational, the payments would be applied to the actual water delivered.

It was a good thing that all was coming together so nicely as the well levels were dropping during this final stage in the process. Again, water rights and ownership are much akin to the story in the movie Chinatown. What was working like a well-oiled machine was like driving down the road and not seeing the sign that said mudslide ahead.

Approval from the Texas Natural Resource Commission was not so easily received. And throughout the year 2000, while the needed approval was languishing in Austin, the Guadalupe Blanco River Authority continued its planning for the pipe line. There was talk of a new dam on the Guadalupe, water forums were held in conjunction with the proposed water conservation districts, and Bill West, General Manager of GBRA said "Barring any delays water should begin flowing by the end of 2002".[16] In reality, it would be 2006 before the first drop would find its way to Fair Oaks Ranch.

By January 2001 GBRA felt it could receive approval from the TNRC in February. All the questions and technical details had been worked out over the past year and finally the pipeline construction could proceed. But, the TNRC did not act on the permit request in February as expected. Instead they scheduled a public hearing for March 29 in New Braunfels to obtain comment.

The entire city council and about 60 residents rode buses to the hearing and voiced their support for the project. At the meeting a number of attendees objected to the contracts. Those objecting to the project cited the loss of water downstream, damage to the trout fishing activity below the dam, possible complete drainage of the lake, and the threat of declining property values if the lake levels declined.[17]

It was a meeting where the guts of all who were interested in the water resting behind the dam were exposed for all to see. There was a definite divide between those who wanted to use the water for personal, landscape, and, with a little stretch, survival needs and those who saw the loss of the lake water as a threat to their recreational and property value status. Although the GBRA provided studies that supported the lake's ability to provide the planned water supply, few whose properties were involved were convinced.

And so the birth of what became a group of vocal and persistent residents who lined the banks of the Canyon Lake took place. This group became concerned that the eight million gallons of water to be removed from the lake for distribution to areas far west of the lake would have an impact on the water levels near their homes. They bought and improved their properties by the lake with the understandable belief that the water was theirs to enjoy so long as they owned the property. Makes sense. It's all about recreational use of lakeside land.

Unfortunately, the lake was not built for recreation. Boating and fishing and swimming and other water related recreational activities are secondary to the purpose of the dam and the impounded water. The U.S. Army Corps of Engineers built the dam during the period 1958-1964. The dam and lake was to serve two purposes: flood control and water conservation.[18]

Following the public hearing, TNRC returned to Austin where they reviewed the issues, considered alternatives and pondered other things that commissions do. And by May 2001 everyone expected them to make a decision. "This is the moment of truth," Mayor Gaubatz said. "I've been working on this since August 1997. I've attended a couple hundred meetings on it. Now it's decision time".[19]

The only decision to be had however was that TNRC delayed a decision so Trout Unlimited (whose stocked trout live in the continual flow of cold water below the dam) could work with

GBRA and Fair Oaks Ranch and others on a compromise that would support Trout Unlimited's operation while still providing water to the pipeline. A new hearing was therefor set for June 20, 2001.

Even if the two sides had agreed on a compromise position, the point was moot. The group of Canyon Lake residents had solidified into a political protest group known as the Friends Of Canyon Lake (FOCL). They petitioned the TNRCC (the name was changed during this debate by inserting the word 'Conservation' after Resources) and were granted a contested case hearing. This action stopped the progress of the pipeline project in its trench and threw a wrench into the three year effort to provide an alternate source of water to those participants involved. Of significant interest is that all the participants were obligated to pay their water supply reserve fees to maintain ownership of their allocation of water once it began to flow. Chinatown anyone – again. The cost to Fair Oaks Ranch in the year 2000 alone was $40,000.

Nobody's nose got cut in this conflict over water ownership. But the wrangling continued for years. The Council made group trips to hearings to plead their case, the GBRA presented detailed information on the ability of the lake to support the diversion of water, and the ecologists and environmentalists provided profuse amounts of data and projections.

Fair Oaks Ranch was even implicated as selfish during this period. Tom Hernandez, in a letter to the San Antonio Express News on Saturday, May 12, 2001, went so far as to say "I am warning residents of the surrounding areas to watch their backs when dealing with Fair Oaks Ranch ... [they] want to pump water from Canyon Lake so they can maintain their lush landscapes at the expense of area residents".

By July GBRA and Trout Unlimited had reached an agreement on the release of sufficient water to keep the trout alive. But that merely angered Comal County officials who saw it as fish over people and a bias in favor of fish that were not native to the area. Despite these objections TNRCC was expected to approve the permit and GBRA proceeded with an Economic Benefit Study and a Water Quality and Regional Wastewater Feasibility Study as part of the overall Canyon Lake water discussions.

Finally, in August 2001, TNRCC approved the pipeline permit. This was a rejection of the FOCL contested case effort and the green light for GBRA to begin the actual physical activity of burying the pipeline in the ground.[20]

Not to be outdone by TNRCC's action the FOCL filed a lawsuit whose basis was alleged procedural errors. They did not approach it on the recreational use argument or amount of water to be diverted. These issues had been debated and successfully challenged already. This new action, however, meant more delays to the project. Of significant effect was the inability of GBRA to now sell bonds to cover the cost of the project. Nothing could proceed until this latest challenge was dealt with.

The Cities of Boerne and Fair Oaks Ranch agreed to split legal costs in fighting the lawsuit and joined GBRA in the process of pursuing a decision in their favor. But it is a long road to completion when you deal with the court system and the battle was still in full swing in March of 2002. A glimmer of hope shined through the cloud of gloom when Judge Margaret Cooper of the 353rd district dismissed all but one of the lawsuit's charges. But it was only a glimmer. The one remaining charge was that GBRA had violated the Open Meetings Act.

It was a last gasp type of effort. The Open Meetings Act was implemented to ensure that no secret meetings of political authority would be carried out. No meetings of public elected officials can be conducted, with the exception of Executive Sessions, unless they are announced and open to the public. So it was that when the actual court reviewed the case, the same judge found that GBRA had not violated the Open Meetings Act and could proceed with the pipeline. Once again the picks and shovels were brought out of the warehouse.

Not so fast there, Lone Ranger. FOCL appealed the decision. And this appeal again delayed the project. A long summer intervened before the appeals court took up the case in the fall of 2002. After reviewing the case, the court rejected all of FOCL's challenges to the project paving the way once again for the project to proceed. Shovels ready?

Not so fast there, Tonto. There is more. FOCL once again appealed - this time to the Supreme Court of Texas asking that court to review GBRA's amended water rights permit for Canyon Reservoir. FOCL's attorneys expected the Supreme Court to support the lower court judges and also reject the case. Therefore, they had plans in place to pursue their challenges in Federal Court. The desire to protect perceived threats to recreational use of property seems to breed tenacity.

The Texas Supreme Court ruled as expected and dismissed FOCL's lawsuit in February 2003, and, also as expected, FOCL filed a federal appeal on the permit. This time they sued the U. S. Army Corps of Engineers claiming that the breadth of the Environment Assessment completed as part of the pipeline planning was insufficient. The Corps however defended its assessment as careful, thorough, thoughtful, full, and comprehensive.

Federal courts are no faster than State courts and possibly slower. The case lingered again over two hot summers until September 2004 – ten years after the Fair Oaks Ranch committee recommended that the City find an alternate source of water. The FOCL again lost their case when Federal Judge Royal Ferguson ruled against them.

It was finally over. Really. Honest.

This courts final ruling was the last to be made in this case. The project could finally proceed and the pipeline construction was completed without incident. The City of Fair Oaks Ranch finally achieved its goal of an alternate source of water with the first drops flowing in 2006.

When a resident of Fair Oaks Ranch departs the ranch via Fair Oaks Parkway, that resident can see a cylindrical water storage container off to the right of the Flagstop restaurant and gas station. When a resident drives up Ralph Fair Road north of the Cibolo Creek that person can see the water pipes projecting from the ground in one of many places on the route.

Chapter 17 — History Of Fair Oaks Ranch

Even on Route 46 east of Bergheim these hook-like pipes come out of the ground.

One million gallons of water a day flow through these pipes to Fair Oaks Ranch. What we don't use flows under IH 10 to the storage tank north of Flagstop and from there to San Antonio. Fair Oaks Ranch, once thought to be too far from the City of San Antonio to be a viable community, is now tied directly to that city to the south and even provides life giving water to it. Too far is close enough now.

But the far out city is still of its own making and had one more big hurdle to jump before everything would begin to stabilize.

CHAPTER 18 – AC/DC

What the Friends Of Canyon Lake reminded us is a well-known fact: "you mess with stuff I think is mine I'll mess with you". It's a well-documented Texas truism that we don't like anyone messing with Texas or our stuff. Whereas the Friends of Canyon Lake believed the water was there for their recreation they felt justified in challenging the Guadalupe Blanco River Authority's plan to remove water from the lake and deliver it to communities miles away.

Another not so well known truism is the difference between an environmentalist and a developer: "the developer wants to build a house in the woods -- the environmentalist already has one there". Most people who move to Fair Oaks Ranch and the area surrounding Boerne are looking for a piece of the country, that very thing that the early doubters thought would keep many from San Antonio settling here. And once here the now 'citizen residents' feel justified in working to oppose any activity that would jeopardize what they had moved here to enjoy.

So, it is not surprising that sparks flew when the City Public Service organization, the utility company owned by the City of San Antonio, Texas, that provides electrical energy to all of Bexar County announced in early 2000 plans to build an electrical distribution substation somewhere in northwest Bexar County. CPS Energy (or CPS as it was then known) provides electricity to a large number of Fair Oaks Ranch residents. Any resident south of the Cibolo is dependent on CPS Energy for electricity. There is no gas service (although a buried 30" pipeline runs right through the middle of the City) and most residences are primarily all electric unless fitted for propane.

CPS officials said the rapid population growth in the area had outpaced its ability to provide adequate and reliable service. Scott Smith, of the CPS Strategic Planning and Environmental Policy Division, said the northwestern Bexar County area was currently served by a substation near the intersection of IH 10 and Loop 1604. The more than 8 mile long single distribution line from that location to Northern and Western Bexar County was insufficient. The high intensity of usage coming with the growth created outages and a level of complaints that was unacceptable to CPS.[1]

It had, in fact grown unacceptable to the Mayor and City Council as well who also had to deal with the complaints without recourse except to urge CPS to find a solution. In addition to the strain on the distribution line caused by the growing number of users, every thunderstorm in the local area posed a threat to the supply of electrical energy. One lightning strike anywhere in that eight mile line could and often did take down electricity distribution for hours at a time. The locals learned quickly not to open their freezer doors too often – not knowing when the power would return.

With the announcement of the proposed substation CPS also announced an open house public meeting scheduled for May 4, 2000, at the Leon Springs Elementary School where they would discuss the five proposed locations for the substation (four, of which, were near the Dietz Elkhorn Road location) and give affected property owners and other interested citizens an opportunity to voice their opinions. The substation would be linked with an existing Lower Colorado River Authority (LCRA) transmission line near the metropolis of Bergheim on SH 46 that would provide electricity available when needed from the Texas grid to which CPS also provided power.

The proposal under consideration was a new plan that resulted from the withdrawal of the previous proposal for a substation west of IH 10 that created substantial opposition by the affected property owners in that area. Therefore, CPS approached this revised plan with the intent of keeping property owners completely involved and informed throughout the decision process. Notwithstanding CPS' desires, the "not in my backyard" and "environmentalist versus developer" attitudes and enthusiasms were alive and well.
Opponents of the proposed power substation and transmission line gathered in the Boerne High School cafeteria at 7 PM on

Saturday, May 13, 2000, only nine days following the May 4 open house hosted by CPS. The more than 100 who attended the meeting labeled themselves the Concerned Hill Country Landowners (CHCL) and, drawing on the experience of others who had successfully opposed construction of other substations, they began charting a course they hoped would prevent the successful construction of the planned substation. Israel Pena, a builder and outgoing school board trustee served as moderator for the meeting. His statement reflected the consensus of the group: "We need to muster enough support so CPS will find alternatives to all of these options".[2]

Although CPS officials said that since Fair Oaks Ranch is centrally located within the IH 10 West Corridor the general vicinity of Fair Oaks Ranch is a logical place for the new substation, the opponents said the proposed sites were at the northwestern extremity of the CPS service area. They believed that CPS and LCRA were trying to position themselves for deregulation of electricity in 2002. Kendall County Commissioner L. M. Holman rankled some at the meeting by stating that "it's going to be built in someone's backyard," implying that the attendees should work for solutions instead of simple opposition.[2]

The next step was a presentation to the Fair Oaks Ranch City Council on May 18, 2000. After nearly 2 hours of the CPS presentation followed by public comments by a few of the more than 125 people packed into the City Hall, the Council strongly urged CPS to consider commercial property in the IH 10 Corridor as the choice site so as to avoid a serious confrontation with property owners in the area. The Council made this position official through a resolution that also encouraged CPS to use underground transmission lines as much as possible. During the meeting Mayor Gaubatz also announced that the City would host a Town Hall Meeting at 7 PM on Thursday, June 8, 2000, at the Fair Oaks Ranch Elementary School to give property owners adequate opportunity to voice their opinions.

Then on May 22, 2000, the Kendall County commissioners weighed in at their meeting by passing a resolution opposing the installation of transmission lines that ran through Kendall County to hook up with the LCRA substation on Ralph Fair Road near Bergheim. It seemed as though everyone wanted to get in the act and oppose the construction of any electrical expansion in the area. The planned development was quickly taking on the environmentalist versus the developer conundrum.

Of most concern to the CPS folks was that four of the five proposed sites would involve lengthy transmission lines in Kendall County. The fifth proposed site would involve a transmission line primarily in Bexar County. In all cases the proposed transmission line alternatives would involve routes outside the CPS service area and within the Boerne extraterritorial jurisdiction as recently ruled on by Judge Ables. The opponents believed existing substations could be enlarged to meet the desired capacity. They also strongly believed that CPS had no business building transmission lines in Kendall County – an area in which they had no customers.[3]

Then by June 7, 2000, CPS had removed three of the proposed substation sites off the table in the face of the objections they had received in such a short time. This was just before the scheduled Town Hall Meeting in Fair Oaks Ranch on June 8, 2000. The two remaining potential sites were Site One west of Boerne Stage Road and Site Five near the intersection of Dietz Elkhorn and Ralph Fair Road. An additional Site Six was being considered farther south on IH 10 and several transmission line routes from the Site Five option were eliminated. The only remaining transmission line under consideration at the time the initial dust storm subsided was one from Site Five to the LCRA substation near Route 46.[4] No one seemed to see that as a major clue as to how things would work out.

It seems it doesn't matter where any utility wishes to put a new substation. It will always be where someone doesn't want it and in many cases those objecting to the substation have a legitimate reason for not wanting it there. The proposed substation called Site One was not exempt from this reaction. Even though Mayor Gaubatz believed there had been a lot of progress and he still favored the selection of Site One he admitted that having been Mayor for 15 years he had learned not to take on fights you don't have to. He believed the people at CPS were trying to do their best. Regardless, residents near Site One vowed to continue the fight.

Not in my backyard was becoming the principal objection to any expansion of capability to provide the essential utilities every one of the objectors relied on. It is a fundamental beauty of this country that we can participate in such objections and influence decisions and in this situation it seems to have resulted in an acceptable if not totally appreciated result.

The end result of this debate was far from over and the

concerned citizens who had been formed in their local areas into groups of opposition remained active throughout the continued process of the debate and decisions resulting therefrom. The June 8, 2000, Fair Oaks Ranch Town Hall Meeting proceeded as expected with the audience listening to the CPS representative present the logic behind their decisions to that point and then voicing their objections to the proposals. The objections even reached the point where one attendee claimed: "It sounds like we need to find ourselves a Boston Harbor" to which the attendees seemed to agree by their applause.[5]

The Concerned Hill Country Landowners meeting was scheduled for Saturday, June 17, 2000, in the Boerne Stage Road Airfield. About 100 people attended this meeting. Whether or not a CPS representative was invited is not known but the attendees were disappointed that none attended the meeting. One person even said "CPS has given Fair Oaks Ranch the courtesy of two visits, but didn't show up here."[6]

On July 6, 2000, CPS held their open house at the Leon Springs Dance Hall from 5 PM until 9 PM. Among the items available at this open house was news that an IH 10 location was under consideration as a result of public comments made at the Fair Oaks Ranch Town Hall Meeting. Whether or not this was possible would depend on the availability of right of way along the IH 10 Corridor where distribution lines were already in place. This possible site now brought the sites under consideration up to three from the two that remained from the original six that were once under consideration. The three sites now under consideration were one near Scenic Loop Road with transmission lines running west, one near the intersection

Chapter 18   **History Of Fair Oaks Ranch**

of Dietz Elkhorn Road and Ralph Fair Road approximately 1/4 mile east of that intersection with transmission lines running north to the existing LCRA transmission line, and the new one at the intersection of Ralph Fair Road and IH 10 with transmission lines linking that station with the existing substation near Crown Ridge.

Various environmental and economic studies took place following this open house and the CPS staff intended to present its report to the board of directors by August 28, 2000, for discussion only. Factors in the final selection included public input, engineering factors, environmental restrictions, land-use issues, costs, right-of-way considerations, and maintenance concerns. The issue became more focused when a consultant who had been hired to consider these factors in providing a recommendation presented his findings. The consultant's recommendation was to build the substation on Site Five - the site closest to Fair Oaks Ranch and a quarter-mile east of the new Fair Oaks Ranch Elementary School.

The 'not in my backyard' approach now paled with a much stronger and emotionally laden appeal of 'not near my children, you won't' approach. The presentation to the CPS Board of Directors was then scheduled for September 25th with a decision expected at that meeting. The Concerned Hill Country Landowners reacted quickly and by September 6 had distributed a letter of protest to residents in the area that pointed out the basis of their objections and was printed and formatted for signature. It included three main topics of objection with the health and welfare of citizens and children topping the list. The other two topics focused on property

History Of Fair Oaks Ranch								Chapter 18

values and the beauty of the hill country. A list of officials in the City of Fair Oaks Ranch, the Fair Oaks Ranch Homeowners Association Board of Directors, and CPS employees was included with this prepared letter.[7]

The Mayor responded with his own four page open letter on September 16 wherein he outlined responses to all of the questions that had been presented. In this letter he explained his position that it seemed fait accompli that Site Five would be chosen and as such he felt it his duty to ensure that CPS would take actions to solve or reduce both actual and perceived problems with the site. CPS agreed to every request the Mayor made during several meetings between the City and CPS. The meetings produced a memorandum of agreement that was written and signed. The issues addressed were:

1. The school problem, health hazards
2. The extensive overhead poles around the City including the substation
3. The tall towers outside the City going 5 miles north to reach the LCRA lines
4. Reduced property values

The agreements that were reached included the prohibition of erector set type structures at the site or along the transmission route -- only single poles mostly 70 feet tall will be used for the transmission lines. Additionally all distribution lines from the substation would be buried as follows:

1. All 1600 feet from the site to Ralph Fair Road
2. 3000 feet along Ralph Fair Road south past the school from Dietz Elkhorn Road

3. 7200 feet west along the Dietz Elkhorn Road toward Fair Oaks Parkway
4. 500 feet north on Ralph Fair Road from Dietz Elkhorn Road

The Fair Oaks Ranch city Council passed a resolution of support for the substation under these agreed upon conditions at their September 21 Council meeting. Not included in this agreement but eventually completed was the burial of all overhead lines along Dietz Elkhorn to the western boundary of the City.

On September 25 CPS staff recommended to the Board of Directors that CPS move forward with construction of Site Five. About 100 Fair Oaks Ranch residents attended the meeting protesting the selection and going so far as to even accuse CPS of failing to follow due process.[8] The emergence of fears concerning electromagnetic field radiation posing a threat to children attending the Fair Oaks Ranch Elementary School now, all of a sudden, bubbled to the top when CPS board member Nelson Wolff shared his concerns in that regard.[8]

The Concerned Hill Country Landowners now morphed into an organization called Citizens Against Site Five. They held a meeting on October 4. Although significant scientific research indicated that electromagnetic force would not be an issue with the Fair Oaks Ranch Elementary School in that the substation was more than 1600 feet from the school and all distribution lines near the school would be buried, the Citizens Against Site Five were not convinced and promised possible legal action.

The CPS Board of Directors (including Nelson Wolff) voted unanimously in favor of Site Five despite a last-minute appeal by those opposing that decision. Many of those objecting to the decision indicated that their new role was to cause as many delays as possible in the construction effort including lawsuits and 'other legal activities'. One of those other legal activities came to them in the form of a district judge's decision the previous May concerning the extra territorial jurisdiction battle between Boerne and San Antonio for the property on which much of the transmission line would run.

Back in May, Judge Stephen V. Ables of the 216th District Court ruled in favor of Boerne when he permanently enjoined San Antonio from attempting to assert any jurisdiction or enforce its ordinances, rules or regulations inside the disputed area.[9] That ruling was appealed and at the time of the substation decision the appeal had not yet been heard by the appeals court. Citizens against site five continued their efforts and collected nearly $17,000 in an effort to pursue legal action. The group's leadership continued to promote the negative health effects the substation would have on nearby residents and children in the Elementary School. As it turns out a specific action by Judge Abel would come to their aid.

The judge's action would follow a CPS effort to inform all affected residents of their activities. The more than 7000 letters CPS sent to its customers who could be affected by the installation of the Site Five substation tried to assure the recipients that CPS understood their concerns and stated that the substation would be even farther from the Elementary School than originally planned - 3600 feet versus 1600 feet.

The judge's action would also follow the Fair Oaks Ranch Council approval of the Mayor's negotiated agreement with CPS.

The action the judge took in November 2000 effectively halted all progress on the installation of the Site Five substation when he demanded that CPS must show why it shouldn't be held in contempt of his ruling in May.[10] The contempt ruling was based on his May decision that San Antonio couldn't do anything in the disputed area. CPS belonged to San Antonio. The transmission lines would pass through the disputed area. Ergo – you're not playing by the rules.

San Antonio and CPS appealed the ruling – of course.

The Fourth Circuit Court of Appeals then took over the appeal of the contempt motion against San Antonio and the City Public Service by wrapping the appeal into an earlier appeal of Judge Abel's ruling regarding the Boerne/San Antonio ETJ issue. With activity on the substation on hold, those in opposition continued their efforts to kill the project totally once and for all. Land for the transmission line had to be purchased and not all of those affected were in favor of allowing such purchase. Eminent domain issues arose and even though condemnation authority had already been given to CPS the objectors diligently continued their work to defeat the project.

Citizens Against Site Five raised another $4000 at their January 4, 2001, meeting and filed a motion with the appeals court requesting it not allow CPS to engage in any activities that would cause irreparable damage to landowners until the court ruled on the Boerne ETJ injunction. Almost 200 people attended the January 4 meeting. The leader of the group, retired Col. Wayne Barth, commented: "So many people said this was over when Fair Oaks Ranch City Council gave the agreement with CPS. Now, they realize it's not over and that they can make a difference".[11]

On January 19, 2001 the Fourth Court of Appeals granted a motion by Citizens Against Site Five to halt work on the project including condemnation activity and then gave CPS a chance to tell its side of the story on Monday, January 29, 2001. That story would be told then and again on February 21, 2001 when attorneys for CPS, San Antonio, and Boerne had their hearing before the appeals court on the separate ETJ issue. Since that issue and the substation had been rolled together and it was obvious it would escalate to the Texas Supreme Court, CPS was going to be prohibited from any activity until the Supreme Court ruled on the ETJ issue. This circumstance resulted in the court itself suggesting that the substation issue be separated from the ETJ issue and pursued on its own merits.

The legal progress in issues of this nature is purposely slow and the injunction by nature of its legal basis was equally slow. Citizens Against Site Five prepared a weekly Questions and Answers document, published a long article in the local newspapers, and continued their opposition. In April 2001 CPS filed a motion to separate the substation case from the Boerne/San Antonio ETJ issue in response to the court's suggestion.

Fair Oaks Ranch, preparing for its first contested election in

Chapter 18 History Of Fair Oaks Ranch

years, held debates in which the major issue was the construction of the substation. Letters to the editor, numerous small group meetings, and other activities in an attempt to stop the substation continued. The only thing that was certain at that point was that any work on the substation was at a standstill.

In the summer of 2001 the appeals court ruled in favor of Boerne on the ETJ issue but they deferred any action on the substation issue since it had been separated from the larger issue. Throughout the rest of 2001 it was point and counterpoint with the Citizens Against Site Five personally involved in their efforts to prevent construction and the issue working its way up the courts all the way to the Texas Supreme Court. Finally, in May 2002, the Texas Supreme Court agreed to review San Antonio's appeal of the injunction. The court quickly sided with San Antonio and lifted the injunction.

The long fight was coming to a close by July of 2002. CPS began to condemn property as needed for the transmission line to the LCRA transmission lines near Bergheim. The landowners continued their fight and CPS continued its effort. It was back and forth for another two years before the engineering studies, environmental studies, and all the other regulatory activity was finally completed and the construction could begin.

In December 2004 work on the project was under way. Further negotiations by the Mayor of Fair Oaks Ranch with CPS resulted in the transmission lines remaining hidden from Ralph Fair Road until well outside the City limits. With the long battle over and the necessary work completed, the substation went online in August of 2005.

If you drive through the City of Fair Oaks Ranch today you will not have any idea that there is a substation more than half a mile up Dietz Elkhorn Road into the Camp Bullis area. You will see the 70 foot poles holding the transmission lines on the western side of Ralph Fair Road, each individually numbered with a little placard at the top and securely bolted to a concrete foundation. The 5000 customers the substation was built to provide energy for have already filled the area with the explosive growth taking place along the IH 10 Corridor.

You can bet your kilowatts that somewhere, someplace there's going to be a need for another substation and this fight will be played out again somewhere nearby.

Chapter 18   History Of Fair Oaks Ranch

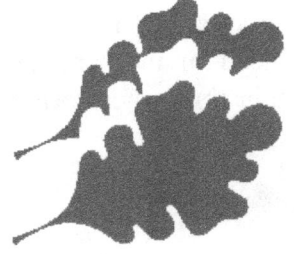

PART FIVE

THE FUTURE

Twenty-five years gone in the blink of an eye. And now the future is bearing down on the City of Fair Oaks Ranch, Texas, with a certainty that can't be denied. Where it will go is unknown. But there are in place measures to help ensure it follows the practices that made it so successful.

The mission remains unchanged and the leadership is as committed now as in the beginning. The scope of activity has expanded dramatically from those early days but it remains mostly out of sight. The size of the City has also expanded in line with the scope of activity and retains the quality of property and structures through the use of specific restrictions built into every new portion developed.

There remain many challenges to keeping this small ship of state on an even course. With the continued involvement of volunteers, that course should remain steady and on the mark.

Part Five

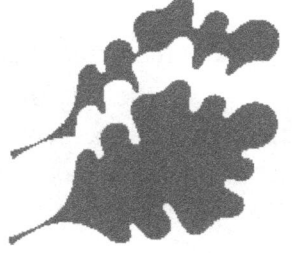

Part Five – The Future

CHAPTER 19 – WRAPPING UP

By the time all of the frustrations of growing up had been resolved, whether or not to the satisfaction of all parties, Fair Oaks Ranch had matured. The adolescent years and the turbulent teenage life span had been filled with excitement and challenge. But after ten years into the new century most of the volcanic and earthquake activity of the Formation, Follow-Through, and Family Feuds had settled much like the tectonic activities that formed the Hill Country had settled millions of years ago.

The once sleepy community had seen many small events that did not cause an uproar or create opposing views among the residents. The small city government carried out its business with little to no fanfare but always in response to the citizens' input.

Over the years the City's leaders granted Time Warner a franchise to install cable television and other communication equipment in competition with GVTC. The main road through the City, Fair Oaks Parkway, was repaved with hot asphalt and striped to remove any misunderstanding as to whether or not it was a single lane in each direction. The Fair Oaks Ranch Homeowners Association relinquished control over the trash collection contract for the City. And the dreaded oak wilt finally invaded the City as it had been doing throughout the Hill Country for years.

State Highway 211, once a serious concern for the City as it was being planned, became a thing of the past. If it had been completed as envisioned, it would have been part of a loop around San Antonio between FM 1604 and SH 46 and would have bordered the City to the south or north. Flashing caution lights were installed on Ralph Fair Road at Dietz Elkhorn only to be replaced a few years later with an actual traffic light.

In another display of commitment to the community, Ralph E. Fair, Inc. donated the property that now houses the Fair Oaks Elementary School to the Boerne ISD and partnered with the City in the battles with the Federal Emergency Management Authority (FEMA) over the flood plain maps. A flood control channel was built to divert flood waters and a portion of the land along the Cibolo Creek was donated to the Fair Oaks Ranch Homeowners Association to be used as part of the Trail network in the City. FEMA would return to declare a portion of the City with houses already built upon it as in the flood plain although they had earlier declared it otherwise. Once again the Ralph E. Fair, Inc. / City partnership achieved success in getting the decision reversed.

The dreaded business use of the land at the City's IH 10 entry became a reality with the construction of a strip center (with City involvement) that included a bar, pizza parlor, dental office, salon, and other small businesses. With the telephone company implementation of a metro numbering scheme, the City ended up with two area codes and four prefixes. And the wooden Fair Oaks Tower, a long standing icon for the community, had to be removed due to safety concerns.

The City published its first website in 1999, upgraded it in 2001, using the volunteer and self-taught talents of an Alderman. Later on the site was redesigned and managed by a technical firm allowing city employees to maintain it in a more real time mode.

The Texas Department of Transportation installed turn lanes on Ralph Fair Road at the Pimlico, Dietz Elkhorn, Fair Oaks Parkway, Keeneland, Meadow Creek Trail, and Silver Spur entrances to the City as well as at the Elementary School entrance. The Kendall County Appraiser was designated as the sole appraiser for both Kendall and Bexar County properties, a unique benefit for the residents until Texas law nullified that arrangement and made each county responsible for its own appraisals. A thirty inch diameter gas pipeline that runs through the middle of the City was replaced with thicker walled pipes because of the proximity of new homes.

Chapter 19 History Of Fair Oaks Ranch

The City held an annual celebration of its birth in the spring of every year through the tenth year. After that the celebrations were held every five years with the attendance in the hundreds as it had been at the first celebration to hundreds at the twentieth.

Three years after that ten year celebration the only Mayor the City had known was stricken with lymphoma and underwent extensive treatments to arrest the diseases ravages. These treatments, including chemicals, stem cell transplants, and open heart surgery were successful and Boots Gaubatz was back on the job with as much energy and commitment to quality as before the disease hit him.

One of the most important issues he dealt with immediately was in response to the Council's resolution to seek release from the 1987 agreement with San Antonio that ceded the Fair Oaks Ranch ETJ to San Antonio. With fifteen months of negotiation and meetings, the San Antonio City Council passed an ordinance retroceding 3,258 acres to the City's ETJ. This action resulted in the platting of the new developments on Ralph Fair and Amman Roads.

On September 20, 2007, Boots Gaubatz' fight to defeat his cancer came to an end. His leadership of the Fair Oaks Ranch Homeowners Association and then the City for over twenty years is perhaps unequalled anywhere in Texas. He was at the forefront of the City's birth and true to his motto of 'Put In More Than You Take Out' he gave his all in every endeavor entrusted to him even as his health was failing. His passing ushered in a new phase in the City's growth, one that is filled with opportunity and challenge. Mayor Dan Kasprowicz and now Mayor Cheryl Landman have carried on the legacy that Boots created. What is coming in the near future is the basis of the next and final chapter in this history.

Chapter 19

Part Five – The Future

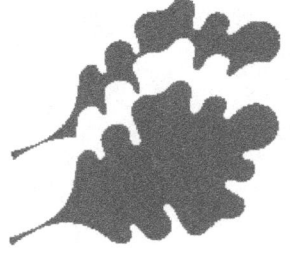

CHAPTER 20 – WHAT'S NEXT?

The challenges that lie ahead are those common to any city. Maintaining a city in good repair takes a lot of effort and dedication and as a city grows its problems grow right along with it. So far Fair Oaks Ranch has outpaced most of the problems faced by other cities in a growth mode. Instances of crime and vandalism are still significantly fewer than would be expected for a city of its size. Limited commercial activity positioned only at the edges of the city limits is certainly one factor that limits undesirable activity. But the presence of a trained and capable police force patrolling the City 24 hours a day is a major factor.

Chapter 20 — History Of Fair Oaks Ranch

With the aging of the City in those parts that were developed in the 70s and 80s, road maintenance becomes an issue. Fair Oaks Parkway has become a major thoroughfare with thousands of vehicles traversing its divided lanes every day. This increased traffic is beginning to create delays at the IH 10 overpass. The deer/auto collisions have increased as well in all parts of the ranch.

Growth in the maintenance and the water company operations has begun to stretch the ability of the facilities to support those activities. The police operations now carried out in what was a long time ago the city office, are maxing out the capabilities of that structure. The fleet of maintenance equipment, police vehicles, and other City vehicles is looking more and more like that of a much larger city.

From the very beginning the Mayor, City Council, and volunteers from across the city have held annual planning conferences to prepare for the future 1, 5, and 10 years out. These meetings have been beneficial to keeping the City in a position of fiscal soundness and maintaining its surplus of funds. By anticipating future needs, great efficiencies have been achieved and waste has been kept low.

It will take the continued attention of both the City's leadership and an involved citizenry to keep the community on a steady course of quality and low taxes. The volunteer spirit will have to keep pace with new requirements if these goals are to be achieved. And new ideas and new solutions to old problems will have to be discovered.

Items not yet in the plan but that will be under consideration in the near future include enhancements in the technology infrastructure. To keep up with the rapid changes in this aspect of city operations may require new equipment and new ways of managing all the data required to support the population and its needs. There may also be a need for a full time IT/Communications employee.

A burning question that needs consideration is whether the volunteer fire department has reached the end of its effective life. Is it time to establish a fully staffed city fire department and, if so, what should it look like? And, as always, there remains the deer problem. A functioning wildlife and animal control operation may be needed sometime in the future.

Some of these things will bubble to the top as time progresses. And the City will always have to deal with unfunded mandates levied by state, county, and federal agencies. But there are other things currently in the pipeline for action in the very near future. The City's strategic plan reaches out eight to ten years to 2020 and beyond and includes a number of must do and justified should do items.

The continual replacement of police, maintenance, and utility vehicles is a continuing issue. These vehicles individually amass more than 35,000 miles each year and obviously wear out in the process. The Fair Oaks Parkway entrance roads are in need of significant improvement as well as a hot asphalt overlay of the entire parkway including new striping. Dietz Elkhorn west of the Parkway is also being considered for an overlay as well, removing the irregularities created when the electric utilities were buried as part of the sub-station agreement. Along with the new overlayment on the parkway, the median will be getting a much needed facelift.

It seems surreal but the subject of a new city administrative building is already on the books. The rapid growth of the City and resulting employment positions created has already used all the available space in the existing facilities. With as many as a dozen new employees expected over the planning period, a new home may be more than just a desire. And additional parking for the increased flow of visitors comes along with that.

Another surreal subject is the Ralph Fair Road over the Cibolo Creek. The explosive increase in traffic on this road dictates that a bridge be constructed that won't be blocked by the next 10 year flood. The expected population of nearly 10,000 residents with many of them north of the Cibolo Creek brings this subject to the forefront.

Finally, all this has to be paid for. The real challenge is then how to keep the taxes as low as practical and possible and still do all that is required. The history indicates it is possible. We've done it for twenty-five years and odds are in our favor that we can do it for another twenty-five. That's what this Camelot does. And it does it well.

EPILOG

Twenty-five years ago I had no idea that I would still be living in the city I helped form. I was involved in raising a family, changing careers, learning how to cope in the private life after twenty five years in the U.S. Air Force, and trying to become a Texan in attitude and practice if not by birth. My previous lives were in constant motion both as a child and as a soldier of the air: seven places I called home in my first 15 years of life and another 15 in the next 30 years. I wasn't certain I knew how to live in one place long enough to unpack the boxes in the garage and attic before I moved again. But this time I believed I would be more stable than in the past and wanted to do something to help shape my future. I became involved. I worked to help build a community.

The glory of it all is that it was successful – almost too successful.

Fair Oaks Ranch is a stellar example of how people left to their own passions and freedoms to pursue what they think their government should be can produce a free and liberty inspired society. The culture we tried to instill in this community is thankfully still a part of the everyday life. The founding fathers had a dream and they turned it into a reality. Those who followed with the same dream made it become more of what the founding fathers had in mind when they made it happen. Fair Oaks Ranch did it right.

If you look into the fundamentals of what made it happen you will see a spirit of independence and self-will. We wanted to govern ourselves. We wanted to keep outside and misdirected elements from telling us what was good for us and how we should live our lives and operate our community. It was a great time in the beginnings of the city that others envied. There were scores of volunteers willing to devote hours of their precious free time to help make it work. At one time we had more than a hundred volunteers working with the City Council to achieve success - one step at a time. It was a challenge and a reward at the same time. We worked and worried. We studied and learned. We kept on keeping on. We reached our destination.

Success has an unfriendly partner at times and usually that partner is not what success had in mind. The human side of our nature wants to tell others of our success and the media wants to carry that message far and wide. It wasn't long before the word got out that there was a great little city in Central Texas that was a wonderful place to live. Taxes were low. It was a liberty focused community. There was little, if any, crime. It was in a great school district. The citizens were allowed to rule themselves. The governing body was not paid a salary, thus no reason to pursue reelection without commitment to the mission.

It was a Camelot.

And they came as though this Field of Dreams was reality. People came here from everywhere. This development too far from San Antonio to be of any interest to anyone began to attract people from California to New York, from Washington to Florida – even from places outside the United States. Many of them came here trying to escape the governments they didn't want to live with in their communities. Unfortunately, they sometimes brought with them some of the vestiges of those governments they didn't want and some of the city life they were hoping to escape. It is a strange aspect of human activity that we bring with us much of what we escape because we often run from the wrong thing.

Fair Oaks Ranch is now a mature city with many of the warts and scabs most cities suffer. We still have a good grasp on the essentials of what the founders had in mind. But with the growth and the changes that come with it we inherent some of the problems of that growth. We now have a few more barking dogs and roaming cats. We have traffic congestion that was once an unthinkable event on Fair Oaks Parkway. We have an encroaching population of country seekers who have come to the quality ranked Boerne Independent School District to find a way to enhance their child's education. We have a growing need to solve problems the founders never thought we would have to face if we could just form our own little Camelot like an oasis in a sea of development encroachment.

The challenges facing the City are many and much more complex than 25 years ago. The space between neighbors is shrinking as vacant lots become homesteads. The once untouched habitat that was home to many species of birds and small mammals has fallen victim to the lawnmower and weed eater. The growth to the south and north of the City has stolen much of the deep darkness the nights held close long ago. In spite of all this there is still the country atmosphere and a sense of self-determination. Fair Oaks Ranch remains a beacon on the hill and a most desirable place to live.

I have found a home in this city and will live here until someone hauls me away in an urn. In spite of its warts and the growing complications that come with that growth, I still like it here. The vision that became a reality is my final home. It is something I worked hard at and will not abandon. Hopefully what we have built will remain a bastion of how it can be done and done right long after I am gone.

APPENDICES

Volunteers

Council Members

Statistics

References

VOLUNTEERS OVER THE YEARS

Trying to list all the volunteers who have served the City over the years is like trying to remember everyone you have met in your entire life, including those you met while on a college party weekend in someplace you can't remember ever going to. The names listed here are obviously only a few of the generous residents who sacrificed many hours of their time to help the City become what it is. All of the volunteers, whether mentioned here or undiscoverable in existing documents, are what made Fair Oaks Ranch what it is and continues to be. Readers who know of someone not included who should be are encouraged to contact the City or the author so any future editions can include their names. Being part of the community is a key facet of our success.

Each of the volunteers listed performed some functional activity. If a volunteer was involved in more than one function, his or her name will be listed more than once. Volunteer Council members are shown in a separate appendix although many will be listed in this appendix as they were involved in volunteer activity outside Council service before, during, and after their term of office.

Because the identification of the various functions changed over time, this listing is consolidated into broad generic identities that are related to the duties each volunteer carried out and not necessarily specific to their individual contributions. Functions and the volunteers are listed alphabetically.

ADMINISTRATION 　　Bob Caldwell 　　Robert Herring 　　Gary Younglove	
ANIMAL CONTROL 　　Lynn Buhaug 　　Cathy Carignan 　　Karen Kelley	
CELEBRATIONS 　　Ray Balcer 　　Sheila Craighead 　　Betty Ewing 　　Nick Hannibal 　　Celia Healey 　　William Healey 　　John Hemberger 　　John Krueger 　　Claire Lewis 　　Gayle Mead 　　Seth Mitchell 　　Jackson Moss	Dilek Parr Harmon Parrott Melba Perrott Darrell Powers Carol Salkheld Joe Salkheld Linda Tom Joyce Turk Ken Wahl Shatzie Wahl Connie Yeager John Yeager
DEER MANAGEMENT COMMITTEE 　　Cheryl Landman	
DEER AD-HOC ADVISORY COMMITTEE 　　Mark Anderson	Jaci Sprencel Travis Wagner

Dean Gaubatz JoAnn Gilliam Cheryl Landman Robert Rutherford	Paul Wallen Craig Wilson Mike Wilson
ELECTIONS Beverly Kasprowicz Gail Cole Darlene Cooper Ed Cross Julie Cross Judy Dameron Rosie Elizondo Albert Ely	Mary Jane Ely June Gaubatz Margaret Harvey Hazel Lander Mary McClelland Catherine Spinella Jeri Tribo
EMERGENCY SERVICES Ron Rogers Jim Buhaug	
FACILITIES Bob Caldwell Robert Herring Wanda Price Richard Wiggins	
FINANCE/TREASURER Bob Caldwell Tom Hamilton George Harvey Allen Schmidt Gary Younglove	

FIRE PROTECTION Gary Younglove	
FLOOD PLAIN Dan Kasprowicz	
FRANCHISES Jim Whitehouse Gary Younglove	
HISTORIAN Pat Buerke Carolyn Hegranes Mike Wilson	
IMPACT FEE ADVISORY COMMITTEE Conrad Fathergill William Henigan	
INFORMATION TECHNOLOGY Gary Younglove	
INSURANCE Roger Beery James Craft Tommy Martin Gary Younglove	

JUDGE
    Jack Peden
    Earl Tracey	

PARKS AND BEAUTIFICATION
    Norman Vestal
    Dutch Uran	

PERSONNEL Ray Balcer	

PLANNING, LAND USE, CODES, ETC.
    Bob Dameron
    David Deleranko
    William Hennigan
    Robert Herring
    Dan Kasprowicz
    Cheryl Landman
    Bert Marshall
    Maxine Nielson
	Jim Phillips
	Mel Sueltenfuss
	Tony Touchon
	Frank Trevino
	Ron Tribo
	Ted Villa
	Rawley Weber

POLICE
    Ron Rogers
    Don Zook	

POSTAL SERVICE Darrell Powers	
PUBLIC RELATIONS Barbara Greber	

SECRETARY
    Wanda Price
    Donna Younglove	

SEWER
    Dick Harr
    Dan Kasprowicz
    Ron Robertson
    Mel Sueltenfuss	

STREETS
    Ray Balcer
    Lydia Beaver
    Jack Bessellieu
    Ray Creek
    Jim Deats
    Frank Hannibal
	Hal Jones
	John Perkins
	Bob Seward
	Rodney Spencer
	Ted Villa
	Bill Wray

TAXES
    Jim Buhaug
    Tom Hamilton
    John Kreuger
    Jim Whitehouse
    Gary Younglove	

TELEPHONES
    Ray Arnold
    Mike Foulds	

UTILITIES/SPECIAL SERVICES Richard Wiggins	

David Hawley	
VOLUNTEER SERVICES 　　Wanda Price	
WATER 　　Jack Bessellieu 　　Bill Finke 　　Tom Hamilton 　　Dick Harr 　　David Hawley 　　Hal Jones 　　Howell Jones	Steve Lynch Don McClelland Frank Shipman Mel Sueltenfuss Ted Villa Richard Wiggins
WEBSITE 　　Jeff Cook 　　Joe DuMenil 　　Donna Taylor 　　Gary Younglove	

Fair Oaks Ranch, Texas - City Council - 1988 To 2013 (Page One)

	88	89	90	91	92	93	94	95	96	97	98	99	0	1	2	3	4	5	6	7	8	9	10	11	12	13
MAYOR																										
Boots Gaubatz	■	■	■	■	■	■	■																			
Daniel Kasprowicz*							■	■	■	■																
Cheryl Landman*										■	■	■	■	■	■	■	■	■	■	■	■	■	■	■	■	■
PLACE ONE																										
James Buhaug	■	■	■	■	■	■																				
John Yeager							■	■	■																	
Raymond Balcer										■	■	■	■	■	■	■	■	■								
Fred Jones																			■	■	■	■	■	■	■	■
PLACE TWO																										
Gary Younglove*	■	■																								
Frank Hannibal			■	■																						
Melvin Sueltenfuss					■	■																				
Rodnet Spenser							■	■	■																	
Lydia Beaver										■	■	■	■													
Cheryl Landman*														■	■	■	■									
Glenn Damstra																		■	■	■	■	■	■	■	■	■
PLACE THREE																										
Richard Wiggans	■	■	■	■	■	■	■	■																		
Howell Jones									■	■																
Daniel Kasprowicz*											■	■	■	■	■	■	■	■	■	■						
Mark Anderson																					■	■	■	■	■	■

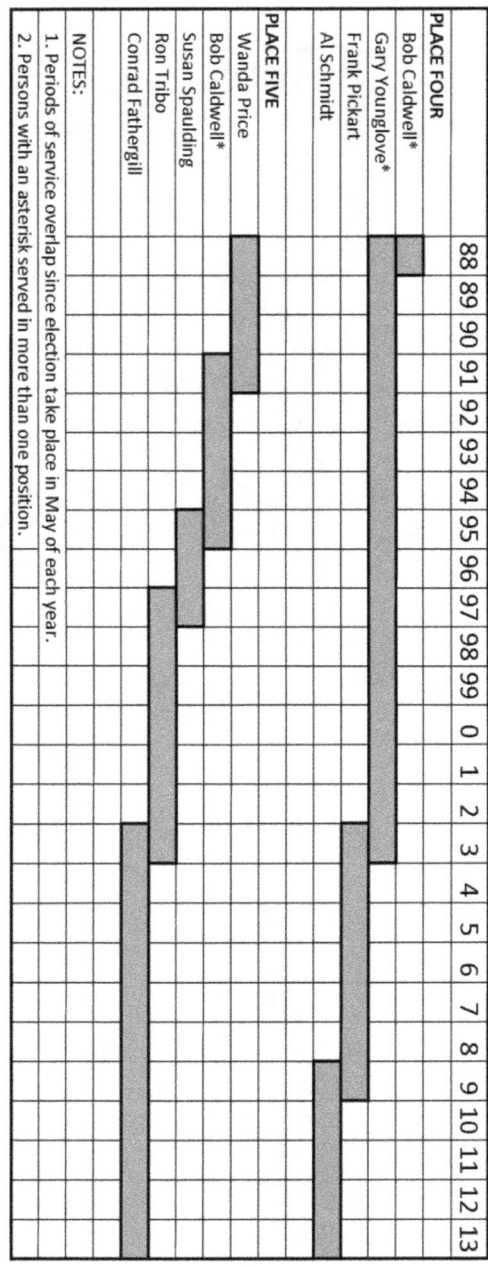

Statistics

This is not a comprehensive listing of statistics that could be gathered. It merely attempts to present a summary of what the small, sleepy community of the 1970 and 1980s has become. Once an isolated and distant ranch few knew about has become a fully functioning city of note.

The entries listed below are a few statistics about this little city. This compilation is not extensive but will give the reader a brief overview of the numbers that make up the community.

Area: Originally 5,000 acres. By 2013 the City has added 3,441 acres for a total of 8441 acres.

Estimated Population: 6,084 (As Of January 2012).

Number of Properties: 3,351.

Average Taxable Value of Residential Homestead: $410,488.

Miles Of Streets: 70.

Miles Of Water Lines: 50 (est.).

Miles Of Sewer Lines: 20 (est.).

Population Of Elementary School: 683 (as of 2011).

References

[Note: Some of the URLs to websites that are listed here are too long to fit on one line. In those instances, the unnatural break in the address is indicated with the symbol →. The reader should enter the address in a browser address bar as a single entry without spaces.]

Introduction

1. http://www.baseball-almanac.com/poetry/po_case→.shtml (11/10/2010)

2. http://www.ci.boerne.tx.us/index.aspx?nid=427 (11/11/2010)

Chapter One

1. http://www.lib.utexas.edu/geo/fieldguides/txtext_ma→.html pg. 1(10/26/2010)

2. Ibid Pg. 1

3. Tucker F. Hentz, "GEOLOGY", Handbook of Texas Online, http://www.tshaonline.org/handbook/online/→articles/swgqz), (11/11/2010)

4. http://www.lib.utexas.edu/geo/fieldguides/txtext→_map.html pg. 1(10/26/2010)

5. Ibid pg. 2

6. Ibid pg. 2

7. Ibid Pg. 2

8. http://www.lib.utexas.edu/geo/ggtc/ch3.html Pg. 1 (10/26/2010)

9. Ibid Pg. 1

10. Ibid Pg. 7

11. Ibid Pg. 11

12. http://www.lib.utexas.edu/geo/txgeo_map_print.html Pg. 1 (10/26/2010)

Chapter Two

1. http://www.lib.utexas.edu/geo/balcones_escarp→ment/pages 21-32.html Pg. 5 (11/15/2010)

2. http://www.lib.utexas.edu/geo/balcones_escarp→ment/images/ 16-1.jpg Pg. 1 (11/15/2010)

3. http://www.kendallcountyutility.com/ (11/15/2010)

4. http://www.lcra.org/water/drought/index.html Pg. 1 (11/15/2010)

5. http://www.lib.utexas.edu/geo/balcones_escarp→ment/pages 21-32.html Pg. 2 (11/15/2010)

6. Ibid Pg. 5

7. http://www.lib.utexas.edu/geo/balcones_escarp→ment/images/ pre1.jpg Pg. 1 (11/15/2010)

   and

   http://lib.utexas.edu/geo/pics/gensoiltxpg1clean→.pdf (11/15/2010)

8. http://www.texashillcountry.com/bandera-texas/→bandera-texas.php (11/16/2010)

   and

   http://www.lib.utexas.edu/geo/balcones-escarp→ment/pages 55-62.html Pg. 4 (11/15-2010)

9. Marshall Enquist, Wildflowers of the Texas Hill Country, Lone Star Botanical, Austin, Texas, Copyright 1987

10. Jan Wrede, Trees, Shrubs, and Vines of the Texas Hill Country, Texas A & M University Press, College Station, Texas, Copyright 2010

11. http://www.lib.utexas.edu/geo/balcones-escarp→ment/pages 153-162.html Pg. 5 (11/15-2010)

12. http://www.lib.utexas.edu/geo/balcones-escarp→ment/pages 55-62.html Pg. 6 (11/15-2010)

Chapter Three

1. http://www.lib.utexas.edu/geo/balcones-escarp→ment/pages 55-62.html Pg. 1 (11/15-2010)

2. Ibid Pg. 2-4

3. Ibid Pg. 3

4. Ibid Pg. 4

5. http://www.tshaonline.org/handbook/online/→articles/nps01 Pg.1 (11/17/2010)

6. Ibid Pg.1

7. Ibid Pg. 2

8. Ibid Pg.11

9. Ibid Pg. 13

10. Ibid Pg. 13

11. http://www.lib.utexas.edu/geo/balcones-escarp→ment/pages 153-162.html Pg. 1 (11/15-2010)

12. Ibid Pg. 3

13. Ibid Pg. 3

14. Ibid Pg. 1

References   History Of Fair Oaks Ranch

15. Idib Pg. 3

16. http://www.wtblock.com/wtblockjr/texas.htm Pg. 4 (11/17/2010)

17. Ibid Pg. 5

18. http://www.lib.utexas.edu/geo/balcones-escarp→ment/pages 55-62.html Pg. 4-5 (11/15-2010)

19. http://www.wtblock.com/wtblockjr/texas.htm Pg. 7 (11/17/2010)

20. http://www.visitboerne.org Pg. 1 (11/16/2010)

21. http://en.wikipedia.org/wiki/Boerne,_Texas (01/31/2011)

22. http://www.wtblock.com/wtblockjr/texas.htm Pg. 8 (11/17/2010)

23. http://www.thingstodo.com/states/TX/history.htm Pg. 1

Chapter 4

1. Interview with Ralph Fair, Jr., October 21, 2010, and his daughter, Susie Richardson, June 2, 2014

2. Rachel Danley, Fair Oaks Ranch Magazine, Spring-Summer 2010, History Of Fair Oaks Ranch: How One

Family's Ranch Became Home To Thousands

3. Ibid

4. Interview with Bob Weiss, July 29, 2010

5. Interview with Don Smith, October 12, 2010

Chapter 5

1. Shared by Boots with the author in conversation

2. Memories recorded by David Deleranko January 2011

3. Interview with General Robert Herring, July 21, 2010

4. Texas Local Government Code Sections 5 and 7

5. Background Paper for Fair Oaks Homeowners Regarding Creation of a City by Boots Gaubatz

6. Pamphlet "The History of Fair Oaks Ranch' handed out at the first City Celebration, April 9, 1988

Chapter 6

1. City Records and personal knowledge

2. City Records

3. Newsletter #2, June 3, 1988

4. Newsletter #1, April 28, 1988

Chapter 7

1. United States Census Bureau, 1980

2. Interview with Don Smith, October 8, 2010

3. San Antonio Express News, March 7, 1985, Section 1-H, Judge say I-10 growth unpopular

4. Report To Citizens Of The City Of Fair Oaks Ranch South, undated

Chapter 8

1. Memorandum on City of Fair Oaks Law Enforcement Services, undated, circa early 1988

2. Hill Country Recorder, May 4, 1988, Page 7A

3. Hill Country Recorder, May 1988

Chapter 9

1. Various Newsletters Published by the City

2. Document on file & City website on January 31, 2012

Chapter 10

1. Texas Education Agency website
http://www.tea.state.tx.us as of June 26, 2012

2. Texas Education Code Section 11

3. Texas Education Agency website
http://www.tea.state.us/SDL/MapMode.aspx

4. Boerne Star – 9/18/1991

5. Gary Younglove – Observation during event

6. Boerne Star – 9/25/1991

7. Boerne Star – 10/23/1991

Chapter 11

1. Newsletter #1, April 28, 1988

2. San Antonio Light, June 1, 1989

3. Newsletter #9, June 11, 1989

4. Boerne Star, June 14, 1992

References   History Of Fair Oaks Ranch

5. Boerne Star, July 24, 1992

6. Boerne Star, July 22, 1992

7. Boerne Star, September 30, 1992

Chapter 12

1. HuntingNet – The Ultimate Hunting Community: http://www.huntingnet.com/staticpages/staticpage_→ detail.aspx?id=365 (February 21, 2012)

2. White-tailed Deer Management in the Texas Hill Country, W. E. Armstrong and E. L. Young, Texas Parks and Wildlife Pamphlet, September 2000

3. Texas Parks and Wildlife Magazine Archives, December 2004, http://www.tpwmagazine.com/→ archive/2004/dec/ed_3/ (March 8, 2012)

4. Newsletter #22, April 10, 1992

5. Newsletter #65, February 16, 2001 (calculated based on number of deer to be trapped)

6. Texas deer glut spells problems for suburbs by Ron Henry Strait, San Antonio Express-News, July 7, 2000

7. Fair Oaks forms deer committee, by Hal Braswell, Boerne Star, March 24, 2000.

8. Newsletter #63, July 28, 2000

9. Newsletter #74, April 4, 2003

10. Chronic Wasting Disease Alliance, http://www.cwd-info.org/index.php/fuseaction/→about.main (August 6, 2012)

11. http://www.legis.state.tx.us/billlookup/Bill→Stages.aspx?LegSess=78R&Bill=HB1427 (March 9, 2012)

12. Deer Management Research Project flyer.

13. Fair Oaks Gazette – Newsletter for the Residents of Fair Oaks Ranch, March 2012, Volume 2, Issue 3

Chapter 13

1. http://www.sarafloodfacts.org/get_not_faqs.php (history of San Antonio floods...accessed 4/8/12)[collected from USGS]

2. http://pubs.usgs.gov/of/2003/ofr03-193/cd_files/→USGS_Storms/floodsafety.htm [... list of fatalities ... TX #1 at over 600] - From Federal Disaster Declarations and Emergency Declarations in Texas in 1998 - Division Of Emergency Management, Texas Department Of Public Safety (April 8, 2012)

3. Newsletter 58, August 17, 1998

4. Newsletter 23, June 1992

Chapter 14

1. Newsletter #14, June 11, 1990

2. Newsletter #14, June 11, 1990

3. Boerne Star, May 1, 1991 and Newsletter #18, August 8, 1991

4. Newsletter #23, June 26, 1992

5. Boerne Star, March 24, 1998 and Hill Country Recorder, March 25, 1998

Chapter 15

1. San Antonio Express News, Jun 14, 1995

2. Hill Country Recorder, February 26, 1997

Chapter 17

1. MSNBC.com News Services (http://today.msnbc.msn.com/id/44441386/ns/→ today-weather/t/texas-sets-record-hottest-summer-us/#) (June 15, 2012)

2. IBID

3. U.S. Drought Monitor: http://droughtmonitor.→ unl.edu/archive.html (June 18, 2012)

4. National Weather Service: http://www.mysan→ antonio.com/news/environment/article/Droughts→ -water-woes-expected-to-intensify-3381513.php (June 15, 2012)

5. MySanantonio.com: http://www.mysanantonio→ .com/news/environment/article/Droughts-water→ -woes-expected-to-intensify-3381513.php (June16,2012]

6. Texas Water Resources Institute: http://twri.→ tamu.edu/publications/txh2o/fall-2011/timeline→ -of-droughts-in-texas (June 16, 2012)

7. Newsletter #37, Fall 1994.

8. Newsletter #40, March 1, 1995

9. Hill Country Recorder, March 15, 1995

10. Hill Country Recorder, September 17, 1997

11. F.O.R Newsletter #61, October 1, 1999

12. San Antonio Express News, September 19, 1997

13. San Antonio Express News, Unknown 1997, Undated source on file

14. Ibid

15. The Boerne Star, Tuesday, October 26, 1999 and Hill Country Recorder, Wednesday, October 27, 1999

16. The Boerne Star, Tuesday, May 9, 2000

17. San Antonio Express News, Friday, March 30, 2001

18. http://www.swf-wc.usace.army.mil/canyon/→ Information/History.asp (November 2, 2012)

19. San Antonio Express News, Wednesday, May 9, 2001

20. The Boerne Star, Friday, August 17, 2001

Chapter 18

1. The Boerne Star, Friday, April 28, 2000

2. The Boerne Star, Tuesday, May 16, 2000

3. The Boerne Star, Tuesday, June 6, 2000

4. Hill Country Recorder, Wednesday, June 7, 2000

5. Hill Country Recorder, Wednesday, June 14, 2000

6. The Boerne Star, Tuesday, June 20, 2000

7. Copy on File at Fair Oaks Ranch Offices.

8. San Antonio Express News, September 26, 2000

9. Hill Country Recorder, Wednesday, October 25, 2000

10. Hill Country Recorder, Wednesday, November 29, 2000

11. The Boerne Star, Tuesday, January 9, 2001

www.ingramcontent.com/pod-product-compliance
Lightning Source LLC
Chambersburg PA
CBHW051750040426
42446CB00007B/297